. Praise for
the
SISTERHOOD

"It has long been both my honor and privilege to traverse the earth and glimpse what God is doing in and among His daughters. And yet nearly a decade ago I was arrested by what I experienced at Colour...in the far-away land of Australia I found a Sisterhood. Never before had my life and ministry been so profoundly touched. I watched as this message spread beyond a gathering of women to strengthen houses of worship. When I learned this story was to be scribed my heart leapt. Now every woman can find herself written in the beauty and the strength of THE SISTERHOOD. Thank you, Pastor Bobbie, for capturing this story so well."

—Lisa Bevere, author, advocate, minister, and
co-founder of Messenger International

"The Hillsong Colour Conference is a powerful example of the strength and sisterhood Godly women have when they come together. What an amazing movement the Lord is building all across the earth through Hillsong Conferences."

—Joyce Meyer, Bible teacher and bestselling author

"We are so grateful for this book! Pastor Bobbie's leadership in our lives has drastically influenced how we see mankind and the role of the church to aid hurting humanity around the globe. Every time Bobbie speaks, she paints a prophetic picture of the church, and as church leaders we are grateful for her voice to be heard through this book."

—Judah & Chelsea Smith, author and
pastors of City Church, Seattle and Los Angeles

"I have been waiting for this book for twenty years. It is more than a message—it is a mandate and invitation to every woman on the earth. I have been personally woven into the fabric of this movement since day one, have seen its global influence and know of nothing else like it. It has helped to shape and frame my life and ministry and is a sight to behold. The Colour Conference has literally transformed the way many approach women's ministry, and has been the catalyst for numerous gatherings birthed from this vision. My dear friend Bobbie Houston has penned the story and heartbeat of Sisterhood magnificently, and as she shares her story, she will inspire you to step into yours."

—Christine Caine, author and founder
of the A21 Campaign

"Bobbie Houston has labored to lead and encourage a global movement of women to understand their value and to make a difference in the world. She has a unique ability to communicate in a way that is practical and revolutionary. Her words are poetic, and her passion is contagious. I know that by the time you finish her book, you will not be the same. You will have a clearer picture of why you are here and a real desire to love God and people. My friend Bobbie is the real deal, and this is the story of an everyday girl who said yes to God and began the greatest adventure ever. Why don't you join us?"   —Holly Wagner, pastor of OasisLA

"*Life changing!* That's the word that comes to mind when I think of my friend Pastor Bobbie Houston. She has championed God's daughters around the world, reminding us of the beauty and grace of our calling. This is a book for this moment in our history. Dive in and join this global sisterhood."

—Sheila Walsh, Bible teacher and bestselling author

the SISTERHOOD

the SISTERHOOD

How the power of the feminine heart can
become a catalyst for change and *make the
World a better place*

• • •

Bobbie Houston

NEW YORK • BOSTON • NASHVILLE

FaithWords
Hachette Book Group
1290 Avenue of the Americas
New York, NY 10104
faithwords.com
twitter.com/faithwords

First Edition: May 2016

FaithWords is a division of Hachette Book Group, Inc.
The FaithWords name and logo are trademarks of Hachette Book Group, Inc.

The publisher is not responsible for websites (or their content) that are not owned by the publisher.

The Hachette Speakers Bureau provides a wide range of authors for speaking events. To find out more, go to www.hachettespeakersbureau.com or call (866) 376-6591.

Unless otherwise noted, Scriptures are taken from THE HOLY BIBLE, NEW INTERNATIONAL VERSION®, NIV®. Copyright © 1973, 1978, 1984, 2011 by Biblica, Inc.® Used by permission. All rights reserved worldwide.

Scriptures noted (AMP) are taken from the Amplified Bible. Copyright © 1954, 1958, 1962, 1964, 1965, 1987 by The Lockman Foundation. Used by permission. (www.lockman.org)

Scriptures noted (ESV) are from the ESV® Bible (The Holy Bible, English Standard Version®). Copyright © 2001 by Crossway, a publishing ministry of Good News Publishers. Used by permission. All rights reserved.

Scriptures noted (JUB) are taken from the Jubilee Bible. Copyright © 2000, 2001, 2010, 2013 by Life Sentence Publishing, Inc. Used by permission of Life Sentence Publishing, Inc., Abbotsford, Wisconsin. All rights reserved.

Scriptures noted (KJV) are taken from the King James Version of the Holy Bible.

Scriptures noted (MSG) are taken from The Message. Copyright © 1993, 1994, 1995, 1996, 2000, 2001, 2002. Used by permission of NavPress Publishing Group.

Scriptures noted (NASB) are taken from the New American Standard Bible®. Copyright © 1960, 1962, 1963, 1968, 1971, 1972, 1973, 1975, 1977, 1995 by The Lockman Foundation. Used by permission.

Scriptures noted (NKJV) are taken from the New King James Version®. Copyright © 1982 by Thomas Nelson. Used by permission. All rights reserved.

Scriptures noted (NLT) are taken from the Holy Bible, New Living Translation (NLT). Copyright © 1996, 2004, 2007, 2013 by Tyndale House Foundation. Used by permission of Tyndale House Publishers, Inc., Carol Stream, Illinois 60188. All rights reserved.

Library of Congress Cataloging-in-Publication Data

Names: Houston, Bobbie, author.
Title: The sisterhood : a modern day movement of everyday girls / Bobbie Houston.
Description: first [edition]. | New York : Faith Words, 2016.
Identifiers: LCCN 2015050564| ISBN 9781455592494 (hardcover) | ISBN 9781478908937 (audio download) | ISBN 9781455592517 (ebook) | ISBN 9781455568574 (international trade paperback) | ISBN 9781455570294 (South African)
Subjects: LCSH: Women in Christianity. | Women—Religious Aspects—Christianity.
Classification: LCC BV639.W7 H69 2016 | DDC 248.8/43—dc23 LC record available at http://lccn.loc.gov/2015050564

Printed in the United States of America

RRD-C

10 9 8 7 6 5 4 3 2 1

This book is dedicated to the feminine heart—to every girl-child or woman who has ever contemplated her existence or questioned her value, to those who have suffered innocently or unjustly at the hands of others or stood bravely for those they believed in and loved.

It is dedicated to precious sisters who have gone before—women who have walked paths that we may never have to travel, who paved a way and paid a price for the freedoms we know. Women whose names may not be known this side of eternity but who courageously resisted mediocrity and opposition, believing that life is a gift, that womanhood is precious, and that a higher way exists.

This book is dedicated to you, its reader—in the hope that with many others, our collective eyes will enlighten, our hearts will enlarge, and compassion will increase. It is dedicated to the belief that together we can understand, experience, example, and champion womanhood as it was truly intended.

CONTENTS

part three
THE SISTERHOOD

PART ONE

• • •

The Beginnings

one

IT BEGAN WITH A WHISPER

(An Introduction)

A number of years ago I sensed a whisper from above—a whisper that arrested my heart and became a compelling conviction in regard to the beautiful daughters of planet Earth (my way of saying "every female"). A whisper that awakened a new era and created a shift on the earth: *"Tell them...* tell them that there is a God in heaven and a company of others on Earth who *believe in them!"*

This book is an endeavor to peel back the layers of that whisper and describe a journey that I could not have imagined in my wildest dreams, a journey that has since proven that when we create an environment that cultivates a divine belief in womanhood, the ceilings and containments that rob so many women of their potential and dreams are removed.

For those of you who don't know me, allow me to introduce myself.

My name is Bobbie, and I live in Sydney, Australia, with my husband, Brian. Our immediate family consists of sons and daughters and a growing handful of adorable grandbabies. We have three adult children. Joel is a musician, a songwriter, and a really tall human being. He surfs and divides home between Sydney and New

York City. In recent years he met, fell in love with, and married an equally tall and beautiful young woman called Esther, and they have welcomed their first son, Zion Alexander Charles, into the world.

Ben is lovely. He is kindhearted and caring and has been blessed with four women in his world—a beautiful wife by the name of Lucille and three little girls called Savannah Winter, Lexi Milan, and Bailey Love. They also divide home between Sydney and the United States. Our daughter, Laura, married a young man who said he fell in love with her when she was six years old—he was all of seven and he apparently spotted her on the playground swings. He says he remembers what she was wearing and that she had an apple in her mouth. He fell in love with her then and there and decided he would marry her. Fifteen years later he did, in a tiny chapel on an exotic, sun-kissed island in Fiji, and today she and Peter lavish their love on a little girl called Willow Mae and a little guy called Jack Arthur. Together as a family, and with many others, we pastor a church called Hillsong.

I am outrageously blessed to be sharing life with an astounding company of people and am surrounded with literally thousands of fabulous women of every age, status, and background who make up this "Sisterhood" that we are about to explore. Their diversity, creativity, individuality, and gifting add color and meaning to life, and their relentless passion and capacity to experience life in all its fullness are unleashing enormous possibility and enabling change to come to the world they inhabit.

Emancipation

However, in an age that boasts emancipation and empowerment of women, one doesn't need to look far to realize that not all women alive "for such a time as this" (Esther 4:14) live with the same opportunities and confidence. The world is complex—it's full of wonder and goodness and it's also full of injustice and despair. There are women on this earth who are correctly loved and cherished, and there are women and girls who are so wrongly despised and abused. A distortion regarding value has plagued our collective existence throughout time and history and has tragically affected many.

The days in which we find ourselves are challenging. On so many fronts the planet we share is groaning under the weight of some pressing unknowns—a depleting environment, financial instability, and threatened global security are prevailing issues that affect almost everyone and disturb the soul of many. But perhaps the greatest unknown is that which assails the certainty, confidence, and preciousness of personal value and worth. Despite living in an enlightened age, many good and wonderful people still question the very basics of life and cannot answer the all-defining questions of "Who am I?" "For what purpose am I here?" and "Why is the world like it is?"

A Divine Plan

A divine plan and dream concerning you and your future does exist, and my prayer as you turn these pages is that the truth found in an eternal, just, and caring God will lead you into a world beyond your wildest imagination. My hope is that as each of us matures in revelation about our own personhood and that of feminine humankind, we will see a new day dawn for countless thousands of women across the earth—a new day not only for those captive to an unhappy or impoverished soul, but a new day for multitudes who are literally captive to forces beyond their control. The sanity, freedom, well-being, and hope of these women hinge on our—yes, you and me—collective awakening.

I hope that your senses are stirred and that you, dear friend, will open your heart and mind and stay with me for the journey. For me personally, it has gently unfolded like a good book that can't be put down. It's been a pilgrimage through an ever-changing and exciting landscape where we have discovered the wonder and romance of being the Daughter of a King—a journey where heaven's blueprint for womanhood has become known, and a journey where the power of an emerging and rising Sisterhood of everyday women from all walks of life has brought strategic influence and change.

I have sought to write about this journey for several years, but in many ways we've been so consumed with discovering and then living it that writing has been held back till now. However, everything has its season, and regardless of how imperfect or incomplete I feel this book may be, it is time to commit to paper something that articulates the spirit of this message and "the spirit of Sisterhood." Ultimately, what has the potential to emerge is a stunning company of women, whose ever-increasing, ever-perfecting, and ever-defining sense of value and worth has the capacity to reach beyond what they may have imagined or hoped for, to make the world a truly better place.

Part One invites you into "my story" within this greater story. A friend once told me that women love to identify. Unlike men, who often want only the headlines or outcome, girlfriends are different. They want to know the where, the why, and the how of the revelation, or the aha moment that caused the lights to come on and the world to change. Have you ever had a friend say, "Hey, back up, babe, more details…Now, where were you, what happened (what were you wearing), and how did it *feel?*"

Part Two is a little journey through the "wonder years," the essential and critical years that framed and shaped the why and the what. Then Part Three describes a time when the stakes dramatically changed and increased—for myself, for our church, for this

Sisterhood as a whole. At that time, destiny and a new era of aware-ness and awakening began to profoundly and miraculously unfold, and the message began to engage (at a whole new level) the lives of those it was intended for. All these parts are intricately interwoven and intrinsically important to the gold within the story.

No end of words now frame this story that began with a whis-per two decades ago. However, in 2009 I penned a declaration that I believe positions us all within its pages. As I launch into what needs to be written, this declaration frames us individually and collectively. As an individual woman, to be able to say "I AM SISTER-HOOD" is liberating, but as a company of diverse and fabulous women across the earth, to collectively say "WE ARE SISTERHOOD" carries power beyond imagination.

A Declaration

So take a deep breath with me as I commit words to paper. I believe many of you will see and recognize yourselves within these pages. My prayer is that as we engage the true spirit of Sisterhood and the future before us, we will realize that we are not only one, but many. My prayer is that we will be impassioned with a desire to watch over one another and be one another's keepers, and all that heaven has intended for our lives will become a stunning reality.

"I AM SISTERHOOD" is a declaration, a declaration about value and identity, purpose and mission. It is a declaration intentional in reach and embrace. It transcends culture and creed, age and status, prejudice and preference.

It is a declaration that positions itself amid awareness and responsibility, concern and care, injustice and solution—a declaration ultimately concerned with the welfare of the world and her inhabitants. It has courageously woven its way through time and history and continues to weave itself across our lives and future.

It is our collective here and now—and it belongs to any feminine soul who somehow believes that she was born for more than what is temporal and fleeting. It's for women of all ages and backgrounds, of every personality and style, color and vibrancy. It's for the bold and bodacious, the demure and unassuming. It's the Sisterhood that perhaps heaven imagined when a very intentional Creator created His girls. It's strong and beautiful, feminine and gracious, authoritative and gentle, and above all else, it welcomes the broken, discarded, and forgotten.

Whichever way it is seen or understood, it is a growing movement of women across the earth—a movement of down-to-earth and normal women whose desire is to take what is in their hand and genuinely use it for good—a movement of women united in heart and spirit who believe that together we can make the world a better place.

With love and affection,
Bobbie

two

A BRANDING IRON

(A Divine Moment)

I was the daughter of slightly older parents—my mum actually had me at forty-three years of age. She had been desperately ill for several years and, of course, the prognosis for well-being was to have another child. So that's what my parents did. They had another baby, and apparently, when the health of my fair-skinned, auburn-haired, and gentle-spirited mother was further threatened, my father refused to allow the doctors to abort this prescribed and special baby.

As a child and teenager, there was nothing within me that sought public attention or profile. I have gorgeous friends who as children dreamed of being astronauts or stars on the stage, but by nature I was extremely shy, retiring, and happy to be in the background. Even now, as the wife of a well-known pastor and leader of a prominent church, I can still easily slip into the realm of "reluctant leader" and allow others to take the spotlight. It is only my convictions about certain things that push me over the line and compel me to stand up and speak up.

So to find myself speaking into the lives of others and entrusted with a directive that has grown into a movement of women of all ages and backgrounds around the world is *hilarious*, to say the least. But having said that, there was always something deep within me, even as a little girl, that knew my life would be overshadowed with favor and that it would contribute to something noble.

A Heartbeat Moment

I got radically saved at fifteen. I was completely clueless that the "God world" I now know and love existed. I was christened in the Anglican Church but my dear parents were not regular church people. They were exceptionally good people, who selflessly gave my sister and me a solid foundation to build our lives upon, but as a family we did not attend church. Often, however, that deeper longing for something more found me leaning toward what was eternal. So at fifteen, when a friend invited me to a Sunday-evening service at her church, my little heart quickly responded. Not only did I respond to her invitation, I also responded when I felt God knock on the door of my heart.

Amid an ocean of tears that rolled down my face and an appeal to entrust my life to Christ, I threw the door wide open and began my personal journey of salvation and discovery. On a clear, crisp autumn evening in Auckland, New Zealand, I gave my life to Jesus Christ. In a heartbeat moment and with a heartfelt prayer, my eyes opened, my heart understood, my past was forgiven, my future was sealed, and I began down a path of discovering who I am, why I am alive, and what I have been called to.

Not long after that, something happened that would shape my life in the context of the Sisterhood—a moment that added a quickening and a glimpse within my spirit to the whisper I have briefly described.

I can't recall if I was fifteen or sweet sixteen, but somewhere in those early days of my newfound faith I found myself reading the book of Micah in the Old Testament of the Bible. I was a new believer and everything about the Bible was profoundly exciting. When I made my decision to follow this newly discovered Savior,

I had found a "confirmation Bible" in our house. I think it was my sister's. She wasn't particularly interested in her baby sister's new-found faith, so she wouldn't have known that I had quietly commandeered it as my first-ever Bible. I remember the day I decided to trade it for a more substantial study version.

My girlfriend Shelley and I caught the bus into the city and made our way to the big Bible shop that was full of witnessing tracts, Maranatha! Music (*the* music of the day), and Jesus stickers, which already profusely adorned my schoolbag. It was the early seventies, and the Jesus Revolution sweeping America and different parts of the world was also being felt in New Zealand.

It was a Friday night, and I can still remember walking out onto the main street of Auckland with my precious new purchase—a mammoth, black, leather-bound Thompson Chain-Reference Study Bible. I think my friend and I went to a movie. I don't remember the movie, but I do remember sitting there in the darkness of the theater, flicking through the beautiful new pages and separating the silver edges that stick together in a new Bible that has yet to be opened, consumed, and loved.

For those unfamiliar with the Bible, the book of Micah is prophetic in nature. For some reason, I found myself within its pages, when suddenly God's Spirit quickened some of the words. It was as though they jumped from the page and penetrated my heart. In fact, it felt like they were burning a hole into my very being.

The chapters and verses related to the Last Days, and the house of God (the church) being so magnificent that people were streaming toward it. It spoke poetically and prophetically of the church laboring to bring forth like a woman in travail and child-birth and of a threshing floor (or harvest) involving many souls. And then, like a branding iron, the words that opened the fifth chapter pierced my spirit in a way that still affects me today: "*Now gather* yourself in troops, O daughter of troops; a state of siege has been placed against us" (Mic. 5:1 AMP, emphasis mine). Gather the daughters in troops, oh daughter of troops.

Divinely Marked

At that moment, as a young teenage girl, I felt divinely marked for something—something that related to my future and the path I would walk, but something also that my young heart couldn't (and wouldn't) fully comprehend for many years.

To be honest, I didn't really understand most of it at the time. All I understood was that these words were like fire in my spirit. I was a brand-new believer with no theological background, yet these verses became so strongly seared into my being that whenever I read them, I would again sense that they were intrinsically connected to my future.

I had been taught that the Bible is seen and understood in two lights. As ink on paper and bound into covers, it is known as the "Logos" or "written Word." For years in our home, a huge family Bible had sat as exactly that on the shelves next to the television. But when the Bible is opened and read with a spirit of faith and genuine inquiry, the Spirit of God will come alongside and make it alive. It then becomes the "rhema" or "inspired Word." It suddenly becomes quickened and active in the human heart.

Well, I think that is what happened to me. God's Spirit, He who knows the beginning from the end, He who knows the individual plans and purposes of heaven for all our lives, pierced my little teenage heart with a divine quickening and a divine moment that would, over the ensuing years, become a revelation regarding my own life and more importantly the daughters of planet Earth. Many years later, the same Spirit would add to that Micah-moment, quickening the whisper I have spoken of and revealing a glimpse into the future relating to value and the well-being of multitudes of women across the earth.

Those ancient verses in Micah actually speak of the coming of

Christ. They prophesy a woman laboring to bring forth a Messiah and the reality that humanity would remain in captivity until He comes. Yet something in the words about gathering in a troop resonated within me in context of a literal company of women within a rising and magnificent church.

Nowadays, we are bold and confident in our statements because we have grown in understanding. Gathering the daughters makes complete sense, and "from a whisper to a shout" rolls off our tongues and has adorned conference invitations and openers. But it was a journey that unfolded line upon line, precept upon precept, and chapter upon chapter.

A Story Within His Story

Gathering the daughters has become a beautiful story within His— a story that in His perfect timing has swept many into its embrace, path, and wake; a magnetic and compelling "once upon a time" that has been in play for many centuries. And this story remains in play because, while many may now be familiar with all that's been said and done, there still remain multitudes of precious and fabulous women who have yet to experience the freedoms that many of us enjoy.

For me personally, the quickening many years ago that felt like a branding iron was a critical moment that set in motion something that would define me not only as a woman but also as a daughter and woman of God. It was also a moment that set in motion a divine plan beyond my wildest imagination that has in turn affected many. Ralph Waldo Emerson said that it is not the length of life but the depth of life that matters. In this context:

I never knew a whisper could carry such *depth, magnitude, wonder, and beauty*.

I never knew it would carry such *challenge and stretch, embrace, and healing*.

I never knew that at times, it would demand incredible *courage, strength, and stamina* and yet also be the source of incredible *joy, reward, and rest.*

I also never knew that it would become a force—a force that would issue from God's very own nature and deeply affect all it touched. The ancient Scripture and prophecy in Micah had found its mark in our generation, and God's unfailing love story—now wrapped anew in heightened revelation of value and belief—was about to become a catalyst of change for those near and far.

On a personal note, dear reader, your own heart may have just leapt because you relate to a moment in your own journey where you also felt marked for something noble and great. Or perhaps it has leapt for the very first time. Perhaps your heart has accelerated because you are sensing that there is more to life.

As we travel these pages together, my prayer is that God will ignite and water His divine plan in your life. My prayer is that you'll find courage to step out, press in, and press on. My prayer is that the One who begins something profound in all our lives will continue and bring that work to "a flourishing finish" when Jesus one day returns (Phil. 1:6 MSG).

The Bible also says that "iron sharpens iron" (Prov. 27:17). A branding iron is a little different from a sharpening iron, but allow me license to say that God desires that all of us be marked, strengthened, and sharpened in context of his will—*marked* with his divine calling and purpose, *strengthened* for the journey before us, and *sharpened* for the territory to which he beckons us all onward.

"Onward" is a beautiful thought, so let's turn the page and step into my story. I can't tell you what I was wearing (memory fails me on that detail), but I can tell how it all happened, how I felt, where it has led, and the lives it has miraculously embraced, inspired, and influenced.

• three •

I THINK GOD JUST SPOKE TO ME

(A New Day)

*W*endy, *I think God just spoke to me. I think He just told me to create a conference . . . a conference, Wendy . . . for younger women and older women."*

That year, I had just turned thirty-nine, and we were in the Home-bush Stadium in Sydney. As a team and local church, we were seriously pumped because this was the first time we'd taken the Hillsong Conference to such a venue. The stadium seated about five thousand, which at the time seemed enormous, and the date was July 1996.

The atmosphere was electric. A vast array of people (including pastors, leaders, and young people) had gathered, and there was tangible excitement because "the church" was venturing into these larger venues. As the conference heaved and resounded with music and song, I recall being captivated by the faces of the young women in the choir. From where I stood in the stadium, I had a perfect view of their beautiful young faces lifted heavenward. They were singing their little hearts out, and for the life of me it seemed that their youthful countenance was brighter than normal.

Suddenly I felt God whisper something into my spirit. In fact, it was more than a whisper—it felt like a clear and precise directive. And with it I experienced a split-second glimpse of something that took my breath away—something that could only have belonged to the future. In that moment where spirit and soul, intellect and emotion collided, I had seen a large stadium filled with thousands and thousands and thousands of women. It flashed before my eyes and seared itself into my memory as something that I can still see, feel, and almost taste all these years on. And with this sight, the following words took form within my spirit: "Bobbie...Create a conference for women...a conference and environment for young women, but girded about with older women...and tell them... *tell them* that there is a God in heaven and a company of others who believe in them."

The moment was weighty and exhilarating and yet it also felt seamless as it landed in my spirit. It was something my heart understood only in part, but with the passage of time it would reveal no end of miraculous wonder.

It Had to Be God

I'm not one of those people who say they regularly hear God's voice in audible tones. In fact, I don't think I've actually ever heard God's voice in audible tones. I value His leading and I have sensed His beautiful presence on many occasions, but my faith, which now spans more than four decades, rests comfortably in the fact that He speaks loud and clear through His written Word, the Bible. But on this occasion, in that stadium, amid the noise and bustle, the impression on my spirit was so strong that it felt almost audible. I knew it had to be God, because it propelled me into a realm of response that was completely outside my personal comfort zone and natural ambition.

As I launched my little proclamation ("Wendy, I think God just spoke to me") at my unsuspecting friend, she swung around and gave me the gorgeous all-consuming smile she is famous for.

The Wendy I'm speaking of is from Seattle. She and her husband, Casey, were our invited guest speakers at this particular Hillsong

Conference. We were standing together, having fun together, sing-ing and worshipping together, when I abruptly interrupted her pri-vate space with my little announcement. In all honesty, I knew I had to voice it to someone, because in voicing it I disarmed myself from drawing back with trepidation or doubt that what I had heard was what I had heard. Remarkably, the woman standing next to me was the perfect person to tell, because God had already used her to profoundly influence my life.

Background

It had been Wendy whom God had used a couple of years earlier to nudge me over some personal (containment) lines, relating to confidence, that would prove critical to this story.

Casey had invited Brian to speak at their Christian Faith Center Conference in Seattle, and somehow I had gotten to accompany him. Casey's and Brian's worlds had miraculously collided, and I think the tall redhead (Casey) decided that he just liked this crazy Australian with handlebar mustache and ponytail. And for those trying to imag-ine, it was the nineties! So here we were, leaders of what had become Australia's fastest-growing church, Seattle-bound, into an awaiting world of new friendship, new adventure, and new stretch.

As the plane descended through the clouds and landed in the lush green of America's Northwest, to say I was a little out of my comfort zone is a total understatement. I was completely and utterly out of my comfort zone! I recall thinking, while the plane taxied toward the terminal, that if this plane took off again and flew twenty hours back to Australia, I'd be happy. In my travel-weary state of mind, I may have literally imagined the plane landing, rolling along the runway, and then taking off again, much to my delight. Have you ever been in a situation where everything inside of you wants to just go in the opposite direction? Well, that was definitely how I felt that day.

Brian had told me that they—whoever "they" might be—dressed up in the sanctuary and I might need to think about what I wore on this trip (God bless him). Okay, dear friend, we're Australian and we have a fairly laid-back, relaxed culture that for the most part dresses for comfort and doesn't put pressure on people about what is appropriate or not for church. I'd been attending church since I was fifteen, and despite appreciating the beauty of godly reverence and holiness, nobody from where I come from referred to church in terms of "the sanctuary."

My imagination was running havoc with images of "the sanctuary." I was sick with self-imposed intimidation and had raided my friends' wardrobes for clothes I thought might be appropriate for the sanctuary. I joked earlier that girls like to know what you were wearing when profound moments happen—well, on this occasion what I perceived I should be wearing was not in my baggage.

Despite the wardrobe meltdown, that trip was a pivotal moment in my Christian walk. Somewhere in the days that followed, God seriously challenged my reality and pulled me over some personal containment lines that, had I not crossed them, would have dramatically affected the calling that awaited us—a calling that had more than my name alone on it.

The Need

At this stage in our ministry back in Australia, I had been happy to do whatever was needed, but what was needed was about to change.

As newlyweds we had moved from New Zealand to Australia to work with Brian's parents in the pioneering of an exciting church plant in downtown Sydney. Six years into the adventure, we felt called to plant a daughter church and had moved from the city into the outer suburbs of the Hills District to do so.

In those early days of what we would later rename Hillsong

Church, Brian and I pretty much did everything that goes with pioneering. As a young woman, wife, and working mom, I was happy to be behind the scenes. I was happy to be the faithful spouse alongside my energetic and focused husband. I was happy to create the weekly news bulletin late at night when the kids were asleep. I was happy to run the kids' nursery and juggle a young church and a young family, and (crucial to this story) I was happy for our "ministry to women" to consist of several traditional Bible studies led by a handful of ladies from within our sprouting church.

But as I just said, what was needed was about to change, and that whirlwind visit to Seattle changed my reality regarding women—and women's ministry in particular. Somewhere on that trip, God arrested my attention and challenged my heart to step up and take responsibility for the feminine heart within the house!

I'd like to tell you that there was an exact moment in Seattle when the lights went on, but I honestly think it was a compilation of sights and sounds that God was using in this season of my life. I recall another moment around this same period that added to the dynamics of what God was doing in my heart. It was a Sunday evening and we were in a venue that we rented for many years. From the front row, I remember looking up at the three layered balconies, captivated again by all the beautiful young people that were flooding into our church—and again I felt God's Spirit prompt. I sensed him say, "So, they are in your hand . . . Who is going to role-model a woman of God to these young people?"

As much as I love and respect my husband, and as much as his leadership inspires both men and women, he wasn't exactly about to role-model a "woman of God" to our growing world—so as you can see, God was on my case and was speaking to me from all directions.

I came back from that visit to Seattle with a newly seeded resolve to step up and take intentional responsibility for the women in our young and flourishing church—not just "the ladies," but all women from nursery and youth right through to wherever adulthood ended. So to have Wendy alongside me in the stadium at the moment when I felt God drop the whisper was, in my mind, significant!

I strongly believe that heaven aligns our lives with certain people to inspire and help us in our calling. The Bible is full of relationships that challenged and fueled destiny throughout history. God used Wendy Louise Treat to ignite something within me, and I will forever be honoring of her for that. On a lighter note, the sanctuary dress code wasn't as daunting as I had imagined, but I fell in love once again with Aussie culture, which encourages one and all to simply "come as you are."

Inspired

Some may think that I came back to Sydney and copied Wendy—she ran a weekly women's meeting called Wordshop, and it did inspire me to do the same. At the end of the day, we were both church builders, and pastoring precious lives takes all manner of forms, so I borrowed the name for our new women's endeavor because, to be honest, I didn't know what else to call it.

Wendy also ran a women's conference, but I don't recall consciously thinking I needed to do likewise. At this point in the story (pre-1994), the very thought of hosting a major event would have struck terror into my little heart and had me retreating faster than from a house on fire. But this, dear friend, is where God is so lovely and amazing—He always leads us one step at a time, and nudge by nudge. He will never ask or require anything of us that we are incapable of delivering, and He will always enable and empower us with each step of obedience. I hope that thought alone encourages you.

So the first step for me upon stepping back onto Aussie soil was to start with what was "in my hand."

We had a young church and a handful of "ladies' Bible studies" that were actually fulfilling their purpose, but they needed to be seriously *restructured, reworked,* and more importantly, *re-envisioned* for what lay ahead and for what God intended.

For the record, Bible studies are amazing and critical in the discipleship of hearts. We are a local church, and small groups have always been the backbone of our Hillsong house and always will be. But our little ladies' Bible-study groups needed to come out from the willing hands of some lovely willing women into the hands and leadership of a now-willing mother in the house. Back in the day, I didn't see myself as "the mother in the house"—and I certainly wouldn't have called myself that—but I actually was. Brian and I were leading our church together, and because God operates through godly and biblical order, a new order needed to be established if the magnitude of the whisper and breadth of that expansive glimpse into the future were to be realized. This little "senior pastor's wife" needed to step up and step out.

A New Wineskin

In what I believe was God's perfect timing, I took a deep breath and stepped out to impart new vision to the women in my world.

As I look back, I see that this moment in our history was probably in many ways our initial testing ground. Perhaps heaven needed to see if we could fathom obedience and be faithful to the foundations upon which God wanted to build. If I could respond faithfully to this initial prompting that related to the women "in my hand," then perhaps I would respond just as faithfully to a greater prompting, involving multitudes of women.

On a misty Thursday morning in September 1994, I decided to wipe the slate and cancel all we had known regarding women's ministry. My intent was to set a new table and a "new wineskin" for our girls.

In Mark 2:22 the Bible speaks of wineskins. In essence, it's saying that "new wine" (new life, new anointing, new opportunity, new generations) needs a new wineskin. Old ways of doing things may have served the previous generation well, but new generations often require new ways. Truth and eternal principles never change, but methods must often be rethought and re-envisioned.

I will never forget getting up really early that morning to say farewell to Brian, Darlene (who at the time was our worship pastor), and a handful of others as they set off on a weekend ministry trip. The sun had not yet risen, the kids were still asleep, and the dawn air was still fresh. As I stood at the front door, watching their car begin to pull away, I remember Darls leaning out the back window and wishing me well for the "Women's Vision Morning" scheduled for later that day. I still remember the feeling in the depth of my gut as the car disappeared down the road: "What on earth am I stepping into?"

I was excited; I knew within my heart of hearts that what we were about to launch into that morning and redefine was right—but I was also completely out of my depth. I felt like I was walking on water, because deep inside I knew that what we were entering into was way more than a mere Thursday-morning ladies' meeting.

I had no idea of the beautiful whisper that lay ahead and expansive plans God had for us, but I also knew that there was no turning back. I would remember this initial moment of commitment on my doorstep a number of times in the years ahead, when the grind of the greater journey would tempt me to give up or find an excuse to no longer run with the vision.

I turned around, closed the front door, and headed into the kids' rooms in an attempt to rouse slumbering, unconscious teenagers for school.

• four •

STEPPING OUT

(A New Courage)

Seriously, Brian, if you announce it as a 'WOMEN'S MINIS-TRY Vision Day,' I may have to kill you."

Okay, I have to smile here because despite the above statement, I don't really talk to my husband like that, and I wouldn't really kill anyone over a church announcement—but the language around this vision morning was important.

Women's ministry was not a new thing in Australia. In fact, some fairly legendary women in our nation had given heart and soul to break down barriers and speak into the lives of the women of their generation, and we cannot forget the suffragettes of decades past who gave their all for women to emerge from the shadows that contained them. It is upon the shoulders of these sisters that we find ourselves standing today, and these amazing women deserve the greatest honor for giving their best. However, the challenge I was sensing in my little pocket of time and history was that we were part of a *new* generation of women, and rightly or wrongly, the girls around my age (and younger) perceived women's ministry as belonging to an older or different generation of women.

Breaking Down the Barriers

The generation factor is interesting. One minute you are young and vibrant with the world before you, and then the next minute you are somehow older, looking at a new generation who are young and vibrant with the world before them—and anyone who has more than four decades up their sleeve knows exactly what I'm talking about.

Generational separation happens, but I am not convinced that this is how God intended life to be. If we are not mindful and careful, society finds itself with unhealthy divides that have various age groups seldom mixing, seldom socializing, seldom truly appreciating one another, and seldom working together for the good of others.

Church life, if we are not careful, can also fall into the same trap, with youth only ever engaging youth and adults only ever engaging adults. However, I have to say here that our experience within Hillsong has always been blessed with a healthy sense of generational mix. Our church has always been a fabulous melting pot of age, style, family, and energy, which I truly believe has kept us relevant, grounded, and relatable throughout the years.

Having said that, the thought of younger girls and younger women attending a "women's or ladies' meeting" wasn't on the radar even for us. So for me to launch out and shape a new day, a new vision, and a new wineskin for the women of our little church (and ultimately the global Sisterhood that lay in the future), the language around this morning was not only important—it was critical. Hence my wee threat to Brian.

I honestly felt that if we announced this special Thursday morning as a "Women's Ministry" day, we would automatically restrict who attended and sabotage the vision, because the prevailing mind-set was that women's ministry applied only to a specific group of ladies.

Our church was already rich in amazing women of all ages, but the young girls, the young moms, and the young university and career women definitely didn't see themselves in this mix. And—dare I say this?—some of my own girlfriends, who were fabulous women in leadership in their own right, didn't see themselves in the traditional women's ministry equation either. In fact, when trying to share the vision with some of those in my immediate world who—may I say it again?—were passionately involved in the planting and pioneering of our church, the response more or less felt like this:

"Oh, that's awesome, Bobbie... yay, yes, wonderful. Love, love, love that *you* are doing this... *but*... I do creative, I do choir, I do college, I do youth, I do administrative, I do whatever it is I do... but yeah (*awkward pause and grimacing face*)... I don't do women's ministry... sorry!"

Clearly I was discovering I had some mind-sets to address if this vision day was to work; hence my pedantic paranoia about how Brian (and others) announced and seeded this to the church.

I Don't Do Women's Ministry

To be brutally honest, the above mind-set was probably the biggest obstacle and highest personal hurdle that I had to overcome and press past in those early days—partly because it was how I felt also. A tragic confession, I realize, but true nonetheless.

I knew God wanted to shape a whole new reality regarding women in the church. However, at this point in the story, it felt like I was the only person in my little world really seeing or perceiving this, and in many ways it was still veiled even from me. I was responding in faith to the uncharted territory that I felt God was laying before me, and because my nature is not forthright or aggressive, it was somewhat miraculous that I didn't completely withdraw and abandon the idea.

Thankfully, Brian had heard what I was trying to convey (yay for Brian), and when he announced the pending vision day for the women of our house, excitement had definitely been felt.

That Thursday morning witnessed a fantastic turnout. We had hired a local veterans club, and the women enthusiastically signed in to the venue. This was back in the day, before our church had any facilities, so the early meetings of our "new women's thing" were in a rented room off the smoky bar of the Returned Servicemen's League Club. Girls had to walk past all the early morning drinkers to sign their babies and preschoolers into the kids' program. I look back on those days with fondness and smile now as we pioneer new churches around the world and watch enthusiastic young teams doing church in the most colorful and unlikely of "sanctuaries."

Two hundred eighty something women turned up! Yes, 280!

An Amazing Start

It was a great morning, and I gave heart and soul to frame what I was sensing. I still recall the notes of the message I spoke, seeding the belief that God wanted to "gather, equip, and mobilize" us. All these years on, we still use that language. It hasn't gotten old, it hasn't expired or been replaced by something more hip or cool. They are still the foundational blocks in this Sisterhood story.

Women were excited and I received beautiful feedback and letters of encouragement. One letter even said how timely and prophetic it was and how women were going to *so* jump on board with the vision. The following week...the attendance dropped by a hundred!!

Yep, one hundred! One hundred women didn't come back, and that's where we sat for what seemed an eternity. Shall I repeat that for dramatic effect? The attendance dropped by *one hundred* (one, zero, zero), and that's where we sat for an eternity. I'm laughing now, but it wasn't exactly amusing at the time. It was actually discouraging and a little daunting, but we had stepped out, I had counted the cost, and there was no turning back.

And so began a journey into what it really was to *gather* the daughters, what it really was to *equip* ourselves for the mandate before us, and what it really meant to *mobilize* into a force that would ultimately become a force for good and a fabulous movement of women across the earth. Together, a small band of willing girls in a little local church in a land Down Under began to find their feet.

As God's gentle and ever-faithful Spirit came alongside and led us into the pages of a book in the Bible that had a chapter specific to women, a blueprint regarding our value as women and our existence on the earth began to take shape. This chapter would prove to carry astounding depth, magnitude, and an endeavor into which we could stretch our hearts.

Our little Wordshop morphed into Hillsongwomen, which then matured eventually into Sisterhood—but not before we took a long and strategic stroll through Proverbs 31 (Old Testament, after the Psalms, if you are new to all this), where we discovered a remarkable, intelligent, compassionate, bold, entrepreneurial, and savvy woman who knew how to influence not only her own personal world but also the greater world she inhabited.

In the midst of thirty-one verses in the thirty-first chapter of this timeless book on wisdom, we found ourselves.

Foundations

Personally and collectively, we began to see our potential and purpose with new eyes. In discovering the many layers within this Proverbs 31 woman of God, we also found a compelling reason to unite in friendship and cause. The foundations of a global Sisterhood were strategically falling into place.

Vision had been cast on that Thursday morning in September,

and the initial ground for us had been cut in the spirit realm…
and down the track, that whisper and greater directive awaited us.
In all fairness to the gorgeous girls in my world, those who could
regularly come out on a Thursday morning joined me, and with
each step that we took together, our courage and confidence grew.

I won't lie and say that it was a stroll in the park—it was personally very stretching. There were definitely many fabulous moments
along the way and reward more than we can recount, but for the
most part I had to set my face toward what I believed God had put in
my heart and then walk in simple faith into what was unknown and,
yet again, uncharted territory. Regardless of how capable or incapable, adequate or inadequate I felt at times, I learned to "smile at the
future" and press on. Smiling at the future was a pivotal truth discovered in the pages of Proverbs 31—a pivotal truth that even today
continues to unfold layer upon layer and revelation upon revelation.
Rewriting the game plan and creating a new wineskin took time and
commitment, and it was in this territory of pioneering that we found
ourselves—so take heart if you also find yourself in similar territory.

Passage of Time

Heaven was watching and favor was about to be poured out, not
only on our own church but also on the nation that had become
soil to this modern-day mandate concerning the "daughters."

As a small band of willing hearts gathered week in and week
out to host and give our best to the 180 gathered, God waited for
the right moment to drop the next step. And when He did, we
found the grace to say yes. Within the Proverbs 31 blueprint, we
were discovering a woman who said yes more than she said no: yes
to faith, purpose, diligence, and service; yes to all the dynamics
that make for health and well-being in life and relationships. She
was to become our inspiration and role model of possibility.

Now it was time to find a date.

It was time to scan the calendar, find a gap that would work in our already manic schedules, and get the seeds of the God-whisper and His true intent planted. The welcome mat of our church was about to be well trodden. As we threw wide the invitation to make the world a better place, thousands of leaders and everyday gals from all around the world began making their way Down Under to Sydney.

With time, this gathering of women would officially be recognized as an Australian tourist attraction, but not before we ourselves had cut the ground again with our first-ever Colour Conference. In Micah, those signature verses that I had sensed like a branding iron in my spirit exhort the Church of Jesus Christ to labor and bring forth, like a woman in labor. I've personally labored and brought forth three babies—and none of them were small. My firstborn was a ten-pound whopper, and in more ways than I can tell you, what we were about to spiritually birth and bring into existence felt like another whopping, gorgeous, and perfectly planned baby—a baby that would grow and leave a perfect imprint of God's goodness and glory on the world.

five

A DATE WITH 600

(A Small Beginning)

*H*ey, Holly . . . if all else fails, I know there'll be at least two at it, because I've just registered you and me!"

That was pretty much how the phone call about our first-ever Colour Conference went with my new little Californian friend from Hollywood.

Holly Wagner and I had met in Wendy Treat's lounge room way back on that very first trip to Seattle—the one where I had the wardrobe meltdown and wanted the plane to fly back to Australia. It was back in the days of big hair, high-waist jeans, and groovy plaid shirts. Our relationship with our Seattle friends had grown, and now Holly and her husband, Phil, wanted to visit Sydney on a trip that Casey and Wendy were also planning.

The awesome foursome arrived, and Brian and I delighted in showing our friends our beautiful city and harbor—and what's not to love about showing off a city that boasts glorious blue skies and sandy white beaches? We all got on famously, but it was in a pre-loved secondhand clothing store in Sydney's prestigious Double Bay suburb that my heart knit with this fun-loving girl whom Brian had already nicknamed "Holly-wood."

I'd like to tell you that it was a deeply spiritual moment that connected our hearts, but it wasn't—it was more of a ridiculous moment of complete lunacy that reduced us both to tears and hysterical snorting on the floor. I don't think anyone else in the store quite understood what had so randomly taken our fancy, but it seeded and sealed a friendship that we would come to refer to as "forever."

It was out of this place of newfound friendship and laughter that I invited Holly to be our first-ever guest speaker at our first-ever Colour Conference...and hence the phone call saying that if no one else turned up, signed up, bought in, cared, or registered, there would at least be two on the record.

A Date with Destiny

Our first date with destiny actually ended up being a date with 600 others!

Six hundred beautiful women, girls, friends, and team joined Holly and me and became the seed of both Colour and what would grow over the next two decades to become the beautiful and expansive Colour Sisterhood. Six hundred and one friends cut the ground with me and put us on the first page of what I honestly believe was a new chapter for women, not only in our own city and nation but in the greater Body of Christ. Our own church, and the churches of so many around the world who would lean enthusiastically into this message, would never be the same. Although we weren't fully aware at the time of all that was to unfold, the fruit has since proven that something wonderful and lasting was being birthed.

All small beginnings look different, and as the wisdom of the Bible says, no small beginning should ever be despised (see Zech. 4:10).

I am completely aware that, to many, 602 people may not sound like a small beginning (especially when statistics tell us that the average church in the world numbers under a hundred), but it's not a question of how big or small the actual seed or beginning is:

It's the potential within the seed and what God ultimately intends for it that matters. Even all these years on, I still believe that God continues to water the same "destiny seed" that was originally planted within people all that time ago. It takes time for a seedling to germinate, take root, emerge, and then mature into what God intended—and I've noticed that for those who continue to do the journey with us year after year and lean into what originally inspired them, the anointing within the Colour environment continues to prepare them for what lies ahead.

Hilarious Memories

Small beginnings are full of defining moments and fond memories that mustn't be forgotten. If you are pioneering new adventures or experiencing the newness of ministry, don't ever fail to remember the crazy, fun, mad moments. At the time, they may seem embarrassing or just plain awful, but down the track they are the things that make for priceless camaraderie, endearment, and heartwarming comic relief when needed. This first-ever gathering was full of hilarious moments, mostly because we didn't have a clue what we were doing.

I remember Brian asking if I had ever heard Holly teach. It was actually a fair question—I think I raised an eyebrow or two and said, "Ummm, no...I just like her."

Holly is now a brilliant communicator, but on the opening night of that first conference I think she just ran out of things to say, because she stopped rather abruptly and handed the microphone back to me. I didn't really know what to say either, but I was the host so I had to say something. I can still remember the blur (and slight panic) as I seized both the moment and the outstretched microphone and in faith walked around this humble inaugural gathering, trying to frame our first meeting. That night, I climbed into bed and I remember Brian patting me gently on the shoulder and saying, "I was really, really, really proud of you tonight." As I lay there exhausted, excited, happy, and possibly a bit traumatized, I remember thinking, "He's just being nice!"

On the subject of communication, Christine Caine, who is one of my dearest friends, an acclaimed speaker, and one of my closest allies in this Sisterhood story, preached a message (possibly her first ever in this context), and I think she completely forgot to use the Bible. She pretty much preached from a teenage fashion magazine called *Dolly*. What she said was amazing, passionate, and appropriate, and it would have been in context of protecting the youthfulness of our youth. We smile now at how new we were to all of this, and how naive. She has since told me that she spoke about a "sealed section" in the middle of the magazine. Relax... she never unsealed it, but suffice to say the content about male genitalia was completely inappropriate for teenage girls. I think I may have suffered selective amnesia, because I seriously don't remember that portion of her message... or perhaps I was still recovering from the hilarious trauma of asking two hundred older women, earlier in the day, to carry their own chairs up a flight of stairs to the room we had allocated for the "Over 40 and Fabulous Workshop"—a room that had no air-conditioning as the mercury rose into the high 90s.

Our church is known these days for its hospitality, and we have amazing volunteer teams who use their gifts to prepare beautiful meals so our guests don't starve during events. Yep, the night of our first-ever Colour opening, I completely forgot to feed my first-ever guest speaker—later, I found her in her underwear and socks in my pantry, demolishing a bowl of cereal. I have since discovered that Holly is somewhat like a newborn baby—you have to feed her every three hours. There was of course no budget for hotel accommodation, so she stayed in our home in my new guest room, which at the time had no curtains. Not a problem, except for the workmen next door who had a bird's-eye view of Sleeping Beauty the next morning.

I found the poor girl standing on a chair by the window, hanging a red gingham picnic cloth she'd found in my linen closet for privacy.

I remember our drive to the venue. Back in 1997, we didn't have our own church facilities, so we had hired the premises of another local church, which met in a factory. We worked our tails off trying to transform it and make it appropriate for a women's event. As Holly and I approached the venue, we passed a humble, somewhat lonely and forlorn-looking sandwich-board sign on the traffic circle outside that read: WELCOME TO COLOUR YOUR WORLD WOMEN'S CONFERENCE. As I pulled into the factory driveway, I silently looked at Holly with that wide-eyed, freaked-out, kangaroo-in-the-headlights, oh-my-goodness look—it was official and there was no turning back!

I remember a line of women—Dear Lord, we had a line! Women were *lining up*. I knew they would be lining up, because (hello) I had invited them and they had responded, but it still shocked me. Even now, lines still make me take a deep breath, which is my cue for Jesus to know that I *really* need Him to turn up!

I remember Deb—fabulous Deb who was one of my faithful Wordshop girls. As I walked past Deb, who was in the line, she exclaimed rather loudly, "Bobbie! Bobbie! Bobbie! *It's a conference!!!!*"

"Yes, Deb, I've been trying to tell you this for weeks. It's not just a normal Wordshop. It's a conference." For darling Deb, the penny was dropping—in fact for many, the penny was about to drop. God was about to open more than just my eyes to the possibilities He knew were within this beginning.

I Get It, Bobbie

The weekend is full of memories that now make us smile but, funny moments aside, the most profound memory is of a young Bec Wood. Bec had grown up in our church, she had babysat my own little girl, and now she was a beautiful young woman in our youth group. I remember her coming up to me at the end of the last evening. Women were milling and not wanting to go home, the team were trying to reassemble the church we had borrowed, and Bec grabbed me with both urgency and excitement and said words that I will never forget: "*I get it, Bobbie, I get it, I get it!*"

She'd gotten it. Something had penetrated her heart and she had caught a glimpse of what it was about and how it affected her as a young woman.

Going into that first Colour, I had made a special visit to our Saturday-night youth group, and to the best of my ability had tried to seed into the wide-eyed young women present that this was their future. It wasn't just a ladies' conference hosted by Pastor Bobbie for their dear mommas and aunties—it belonged also to them. And—this was a big and—if they could catch sight of the vision, they would also be the ones who would carry this message of value to a threatened and rapidly imploding generation.

Micah chapter 5 speaks of a "state of siege" (Mic. 5:1 AMP) being laid against humanity. Down through time and history, that siege has come in many forms, but one of the most relentless attacks against humanity has been in an unreasonable oppression and distortion of value of women. From the outset of time, mankind's spiritual enemy (aka Lucifer, Satan, Devil, Accuser, Adversary, Liar and Thief) has held God's daughters in contempt and hatred.

It is a contempt and hatred that over the centuries has taken many forms. At times it has been simply unfair and wrong, and at times it has been so outrageous and so insidious that one wonders how human beings can perpetrate such evil against one another.

Society officially calls it "misogyny," the hatred of women—and sadly, it is alive and flourishing, even in many so-called modern and sophisticated societies. It is a hatred that birthed at the beginning of history with the fall of mankind and its consequence, and

I believe it is retaliation by the enemy, because he knows—and is deeply afraid of—the unharnessed potential of a woman.

A New Day

What we were embarking on with the launch of the Colour message wasn't just a chick-party picnic in the park. What we were heading toward was a full-scale response to all that had historically assailed the value and worth of women. Not only were women about to be enlightened, men also were about to embark on a new chapter. They were about to see their wives and daughters, sisters and mothers in a new light that would ultimately bear astonishing fruit.

The men were getting it, the women were getting it, and most importantly, the enemy and adversary of the human soul was about to get it! His long-existing plans to destroy the value and potential of women were about to be seriously challenged by a small but rising army of women.

These were early days, but a new day was dawning. A new belief was taking root within us, and any age barriers that had historically separated young and older women had been broken in this first gathering. We had harnessed the language of "together." We didn't fully comprehend how strategically knit this Sisterhood was going to become, but we had taken our first-ever small-beginning conference and given the best we had to offer. God accepted our humble offering and perhaps leaned back on His big old throne knowing that we had chosen obedience—and more importantly, would continue to choose obedience. Suddenly the first chapter was written, with the Spirit of God poised and ready to blow open the next.

Psalm 112:4 (ESV) says, "Light dawns in the darkness for the upright; he is gracious, merciful, and righteous." A new day of placing value upon womanhood and shining heightened light into the darkness had dawned.

six

WHAT'S IN A NAME?

(A New Authority)

So Bobbie, can we ask—what made you call it Colour?"

People are intrigued by different things and therefore ask different questions—and back in the day, this one was obviously a point of intrigue because the question was frequently asked.

Names are important. They tell a story and they paint a picture.

My real name is actually Roberta. Not many people call me that—Brian does on occasion when he's trying to get my attention, and occasionally certain friends refer to me as "Roberta Lee." Roberta Lee Houston—say it with a lovely broad Southern accent and I feel like I should have cowboy boots and a horse stashed somewhere. My parents were apparently expecting a son and had confidently told the hospital staff that he would be called Robert. When the bundle ended up being pink rather than blue, the hospital staff took it upon themselves to add an "a" and wrote ROBERTA above the crib, and that's apparently the story behind my name— world-changing trivia that could come in handy if you ever find me daydreaming into space and need to arrest my attention.

When it came to naming this "chick" gathering, I'd really like to say that it was another divine moment, but it wasn't.

Mine to Discover

What God had deposited within my heart to create was definitely inspired from above, but the naming of it was mine to discover. As human beings we're actually in a creative partnership with God. There are some aspects that we *must* wait for, but once we have clarity, I truly believe that our Father in heaven leaves the creativity up to us, a paintbrush in hand and more or less says, "Okay, start coloring and let's see what emerges on the canvas." I don't know what God has intended for the canvas of your life, but I'm confident the same principle applies to you. Sometimes we simply need to step out in faith and trust our own instincts, knowing that God is well able to guide and correct should we start coloring outside the lines He has ordained.

The actual name (Colour) was inspired by—dare I confess this?—a fashion mag!

Now, back in the day, this was possibly *not* what some people expected to hear when the spiritual question was posed. I vaguely recall a couple of slightly shocked faces in the crowd when I was once asked this question on a panel. However, to the vast majority it was a delightfully refreshing answer.

I had been browsing through *Vogue* and had seen the words "color your world." The words must have unconsciously resonated, and somehow that is what I decided to call the conference. The idea of coloring one's world was way more appealing than a bland heading that merely read WOMEN'S CONFERENCE. I share this little detail of the story because, over the years, I've discovered that God is always a reassuring step ahead in all we are entering into.

Actually, He is way more than a step ahead—He's light-years ahead and masterful at joining the dots in His master plan, which weaves itself around and through all our lives. In the same way that a natural parent delights in watching a child learn to walk, God delights in watching you and me engage the stepping-stones that He has already ordained and perfectly positioned before us.

The Bible teaches that the thoughts and the plans He has for us He has had since the foundations of the earth (see Jer. 29 and Eph. 1). I may have stumbled across the name "Colour" flicking through a fashion mag on a lazy, hazy afternoon in Oz, but I was soon to discover that God was quietly overshadowing each little step and flick of the page. A powerful truth was about to be entered into, and the naming of this event had a strategic part to play in it.

Manifold

The plot thickened as I was reading my Bible not long thereafter. The text on the open page of my much-loved Amplified Bible spoke of the grace of God and it used the word "manifold" to describe that grace. I typed that word into the study program of my computer and waited. There before my eyes materialized the most beautiful description, which would capture my heart, affirm all I was sensing, and confirm that the name of our conference was indeed heaven-inspired and prophetic.

The word "manifold" has been described as the many tints and hues and *colorful expressions of God* entering the human arena. When I read this, my heart totally skipped a beat. Listen to these words again . . . the many tints and hues and colorful, colorful, colorful expressions of God, entering the human arena. How divine, how beautiful, how profound, how perfect—suddenly I saw our little conference in a different light.

I saw us coloring and influencing our world with the many tints and hues and colorful expressions of heaven above and God Himself. I saw us as women, walking His tangible grace and glory into a broken and hurting world. And I saw us coloring the suburbs, cities—the entire planet, for that matter—with the very real and felt goodness of God.

The conference was already an invitation to make the world a better place, and we would make it a better place by carrying heaven's tangible and undeniable goodness into the lives of the people we encountered. It made perfect sense. I was yet again overwhelmed at how gracious God was in allowing me to gently unearth these truths in my own heart first. I committed the definition to memory and have for many years now always found a way to seed it into the hearts of women and girls joining the journey.

Word Began to Spread

For centuries, religion that carries little life has drained the color from the true Christian experience. God is actually the "author of life" (Acts 3:15). Nature silently and yet boldly testifies of His existence, handiwork, and creativity. The planet pulsates with color, vibrancy, energy, and the miracle of ongoing new birth. They say that in heaven the dimension of color and hues is completely beyond imagination. God's character is eternal and magnificent, and there is no end to His breathtaking grace and goodness. The Word says that His mercies—toward each and every one of us—are new every morning…and this Sisterhood, which was destined before the foundations of the earth, was about to become a living, walking, breathing feminine expression of that goodness.

What's in a name? More, it seemed, than we had imagined. We were also to discover a new authority in who we are and, more importantly, who He is—the One, whose Name is above all names and whose authority and rule outlasts and outshines all (see Ps. 8:1 and 138:2 and Eph. 1:21).

The revelations were coming thick and fast as we set course like a newly commissioned sailing ship and launched into the second Colour. This second conference was in our beautiful first-ever brand-new church building. I invited Holly again, and this time also our dear friend Wendy. I wanted to honor her and have her inspire women in the same way that she had inspired me. We grew that second year from 602 to a shade under one thousand, and word began to spread.

Hillsong was already regarded and respected by others as a leader church. God had graced our house with a clear directive to champion the church or, more specifically, to champion the cause of the local church everywhere.

Our music and worship were being sung and embraced by a broad spectrum of the Body of Christ around the world, and we were familiar with hosting visitors at our annual July Hillsong Conference. Now this sun-drenched church Down Under had something else on the table—she was hosting an annual women's conference and interest was strong. Pastors, leaders, and believers alike began to lean in and plan a trip to Australia not only in July but also in March, the month of the Colour Conference. Colour was on the map, she was becoming a circled date on many calendars, and God's Spirit was beginning to draw women and key players from far and wide.

In those early and formative years, many would plead with me to host Colour in their city, town, or nation. I appreciated their confidence in asking, but my response was always "No, what you need to do is take the spirit of this message home to where you are from. This conference is called Colour Your World, so babe, you need to go home and color *your* world."

I honestly believed what I was saying.

Hosting these first two conferences hadn't come without challenge and stretch. The thought of taking Colour on the road was something I didn't have the capacity to even marginally comprehend (yet)—plus, as a church, we have a strong ethos about respecting those already in the field. We will never land in a city without first being mindful of what is already happening there.

Having said that, the world is a big place, multitudes are in need of truth, and we all have to realize that the field is big enough to contain us all. We currently have campuses in many key locations around the world, and these Hillsong church plants have only ever added to the city and the health of the church already there. If God decides to add more laborers to any fields that ultimately belong to Him, then let us all rejoice and remember that He indeed is Lord of the harvest. The parable of the vineyards and workers in Matthew 20 has lessons galore for all of us in this context.

However, one day my eyes widened to what I needed to see about the sphere entrusted.

Think Bigger

I'd always encouraged others to go color "their world"—and then one day, like a bolt of lightning, God reminded me that my world was actually larger than Sydney alone. My own words turned around and spoke right back to me, causing me to see that this whisper and message for His daughters was intended to go beyond my own backyard and nation.

For the next few years I held this revelation close to my heart. Our church had already expanded to London and eastern Europe in the belief that we could influence the Northern Hemisphere, and it was now time to expand this vision for womanhood and enter those European fields. That divinely inspired glimpse, way back in the Homebush Olympic stadium, actually contained thousands of women from places beyond Australia, and the Spirit of God was intent on stretching my thinking in order to accommodate the vision. Personally I needed to THINK BIGGER—so to that end, God sent a modern-day prophet to drive these words into my heart and show me how. The timing was mid-1999.

A woman by the name of Cathy Lechner was an invited guest

at another of our July conferences. Cathy had visited Australia a few years earlier, and my life had already collided with her profound ministry gift. She had been quite instrumental in pushing me to complete my first book, *I'll Have What She's Having*—but that's another story.

The weekend after this particular conference, Cathy was on our Sunday platform, teaching and amusing everyone with her delightful manner and hilarious sense of humor. She then called Brian and me up onto the stage and proceeded to speak (and prophesy) over our lives. For those unfamiliar with this terminology, prophecy is a biblical ministry gift that allows a person to bring godly encouragement regarding another's life or future (see Rom. 12:3–8). Godly prophecy is never manipulative or directive in a controlling sense, but rather something that confirms or seeds what lies in the future. That night, Cathy spoke some amazing things over our lives that have since become reality. After speaking to us together about things relating to our leadership, family, and nation, she turned and spoke directly to me. This is what she said:

And I heard the Lord say, "Woman of God, THINK BIGGER.
"THINK BIGGER, THINK BIGGER, THINK BIGGER, THINK BIGGER, THINK BIGGER." The Lord says, "I'm going to double, will I not even triple?" says the Lord. "The women who are crying, I'll give miracles to get them here." Think bigger, for the Lord says, "You thought bigger, but you said, 'But Lord, I have to think practical and bigger. How can I think practical and bigger?'" The Lord says, "I have surrounded you with women. YOU GET THE INSPIRATION and they'll carry out THE VISION. Press out the limits. Raise women up in the nations to know who they are and what they've been called to do—women who understand authority, women who are not afraid to stand with and behind and under the men of

God, but women who will carry a scepter in their hand and a crown on their head. Think bigger," says the Lord, "because I chose you with an anointing of an Esther. Think bigger—the season is now!"

There was so much to take in and absorb, not least the fact that His presence felt so tangibly near. To that end, we always have people transcribe what is spoken, so that we can ponder the words further and not mistakenly read between the lines.

Affirmation and Vision-Telling

This completely unexpected word over my life powerfully affirmed and fueled so many aspects of the Colour journey that still lay dormant in my heart, but more importantly it confirmed the immediate next step. I'm sure you'll agree that getting that next step correct is of paramount importance to any leader who doesn't want to run ahead of God's game plan for their life.

Three months prior to that word from Cathy, I felt as if God had seeded the creative look and feel of the next invitation to what would be our third Colour gathering. I'm laboring these details because the brochure invitations were playing a huge role in helping women to understand the heart and vision of what this thing was about. I've never done a marketing course but I'm confident that "vision-telling" is about helping others to see, feel, and ultimately capture what you are seeing. So in the weekend immediately following that second Colour (during Sunday morning church, when I had every reason to gratefully relax and zone out a little), images of how to photoshoot and craft the following year's invitation suddenly popped into my head. I don't believe it was just a bright idea on my part—I believe it was a bright idea on God's part.

The New Testament book of James speaks of how every good

and perfect gift comes down from the Father of the heavenly lights—and I felt like this bright idea and gift of creativity was in perfect sync with His plan for His girls (James 1:17).

Tiaras and Crowns

In what was a fleeting moment during worship, I saw women of all ages with tiaras on their heads. I saw babies and toddlers, young girls and women. They represented the everyday girls, doing every-day life in everyday clothes, but the delicate tiara crowns on their cute little heads positioned them differently. They were indeed twenty-first-century modern everyday girls, loving and living life, but the crowns identified them as daughters of the Most High God. And if they were daughters of the Most High, then that in essence made them *Daughters of a KING!*

When Cathy pronounced that prophetic word over me a few months later, she spoke of women with a crown on their head and a scepter in their hand. For those unsure, a scepter is a symbol of authority and rule.

As I stood on that stage, trying to absorb all that was being said, with my mind flashing back to this earlier imagery, I felt both stunned and humbled. Those listening and witnessing what was being spoken over their senior pastor had no idea how personal and applicable the words were. They had no idea how dramatically con-firming this prophetic word was of all that was brewing in my spirit.

At that time, tiaras and crowns weren't really on the women's ministry radar, and if they were, I had definitely missed that memo. Tiaras and crowns were the domain of the truly royal—what you visited as a tourist in the historic Tower of London or the ancient cities of Europe. Tiaras and crowns were made of diamonds and gold and precious stones. Plastic and other fake versions didn't overly adorn the shelves of little gift stores or Kmart as they do now, enabling every little girl's dream of being a princess to come true. Tiaras and crowns for the vast majority of us belonged with fairy-tale stories and Disney parade characters.

Stance and Authority

The critical next page in this unfolding Sisterhood story was about to turn—and what lay on that page would profoundly impact the hearts of many.

The reality that we are Daughters of a King was about to redefine and heal the shattered and suffering hearts of so many girls. It was about to change the way we viewed life and the way we allowed life to happen to us—and it was about to fashion anew our dignity, stance, and ultimately the authority under which we live and move.

Worthy of note is that the year we commenced Colour was 1997. Five months after we started the conference in March, two profound lives passed into eternity. Two astounding women fell like seed into the earth within days of each other. Both were princesses and both were advocates of humanity.

One was a literal princess—beautiful, captivating, graced with wealth and influence. The other was also a princess but from a different realm—equally beautiful and captivating but graced with a different influence and wealth. The latter was a devoted daughter of heaven, a true lover of Jesus Christ with an unyielding passion to place value and dignity upon others. The Bible says: "Unless a grain of wheat is buried in the ground, dead to the world, it is never any more than a grain of wheat. But if it is buried, it sprouts and *reproduces itself many times over*" (John 12:24 MSG, emphasis mine).

I am speaking of the lives of Princess Diana and Mother Teresa. I find it interesting that in the same year these two remarkable women were ushered into eternity, a new day was dawning for a great host of women to emerge...a great host of everyday girls who would (as daughters with royal stance) carry themselves with the dignity and grace, compassion, and human touch of these two women.

Like all of us, Diana was not perfect, but her genuine compassion and love for others was undeniable. Mother Teresa was a petite giant with an all-consuming devotion, who relentlessly walked Christ into the loneliness and despair of others.

A Scepter of Authority

Cathy had prophesied the raising up of women across the nations who would "know who they are and what they had been called to"—women who would wear a crown on their head and carry a scepter in their hand, women who would know the blessing, authority, power, and anointing in the Glorious Name (Jesus) that was a banner of truth over their lives. What that Name truly meant and what we were collectively being called into was crystallizing before our eyes.

So I presented the question at the front end of this chapter—"What's in a name?"

In all truthfulness, so much! The message and mandate of the Daughter of a King was becoming profoundly clear. A great host of everyday girls from all walks of life were about to emerge. They would carry their own name and be their own diverse and individual selves, but they would also carry a Name that carried weight and authority, the Name of their heavenly King. With the divine intent of heaven, they were about to be truly inspired, empowered, and strategically sown into the earth.

Adjust Your Tiara

There's a fun poster campaign called KEEP CALM. One of the cutest I've seen reads, KEEP CALM AND ADJUST YOUR TIARA. Personally I don't walk around with a plastic tiara on my head—and I'm sure some of you reading are glad about that! However, the imagery paints a picture of greater dynamics that are often at play in life.

You may seriously have all your ducks in a row and colorful marbles in the bag—and your invisible tiara may be perfectly positioned on your wee head. And if that's the case, I'm honestly thrilled and love that you are figuring life from a place of strength. But this world is tragically full of beautiful women and girls who have no revelation of value, worth, or God-given authority. They allow themselves to live short of their own true potential or allow life and others to assault them because they don't realize that they deserve more. So many women are cruelly—and at times savagely—subjected to things that devalue their true, precious, and royal personhood.

The "Daughter of a King" revelation is for *them*!

It's to help them realize that there is more to life, and that indeed there is One whose Name is above all names. He is attentive to their cry, He knows the complexities of their existence, and He is poised to enter their heart and journey if they can just lift their head long enough to know that He actually exists and cares. Their own gorgeous names are lovingly and affectionately inscribed on His heart, and it's for them this whisper of divine belief was meant.

It is for them this story is being told.

seven

MARQUEES AND ELEPHANTS

(The Stretch)

*H*ey, babe, the venue is full and the girls are having a meltdown! They've left it too late and MISSED OUT!"

This was one of those famous hallway conversations that happen in busy churches among busy teams.

Colour ONE with 602 in attendance was under our belt, Colour TWO with nearly a thousand cute bottoms on seats had been a great success, and now Colour THREE—shock, horror—had filled up before a stack of our own local girls had even registered. I had heard via the grapevine that a few of them were "dissolving into despair" over the fact that they had missed out. Apparently there were some seriously unhappy, disappointed, and marginally shocked girls floating around our little city and beyond.

It was to Brian that I had directed my remark. He was in the hallway, headed downstairs, when I presented my dilemma. He paused, hand on the glass door of our third-level offices, and said in his deep, male, gravelly voice, "Get a tent!"—and then proceeded through the door and off to wherever he was going.

I stood there somewhat frozen as he disappeared down the stairs. Did he just say get a tent? Get a *tent!* What does that mean? How on earth do I know how to get a tent?

Surrounded

Well, dear friends, it was in this fleeting moment on a stairwell that I quickly realized that none of us are supposed to be figuring destiny alone. The stretch of the adventure and the stretch of calling will extend all of us in different ways. The cute prophet with the zany sense of humor had prophesied that, as I obeyed and thought *bigger*, God had already surrounded me with women, and that, as I allowed the inspiration to take shape in my heart, *they* would help "carry out the vision."

That encouraging word wasn't gender-specific to women only. Over the coming years, it would not only be a brilliant team of women who would make the vision reality, it would also involve many amazing men who would align and add their strength. So that year, we stretched our fledgling capacity and advertised that, yay, in addition to filling the Hub Auditorium, which seated a good fifteen hundred, we would also have a *live second conference happening at the same time* in a tent—a tent that would enable another thousand women to attend!

After thirteen years of renting venues, we had just built our first new church building, and there was space allocated for a parking lot that hadn't yet been developed. According to Brian and the lads, it was a perfect parcel of dirt upon which we could erect the tent. The only problem: The land wasn't exactly level. So someone organized some willing landscape guys in our church to level the ground for our first-ever marquee tent—another signature first-ever! I must say that we love the volunteer spirit that lends a hand when needed. We deeply appreciated the gracious offer, and the lovely landscape lads did a great job—almost! (More of that later...)

In context of recalling how we were stretching to become tent experts, I remember a few years earlier we had attempted a tent crusade when we first secured the land for the new building. A tent crusade would build faith and give everyone a taste of having church on the literal land that we had all stretched and sacrificed to purchase. At the time, I had personally (and perhaps naively) visualized the kind of tent that old-time revivalists used—big, white, exciting, with the evening sun romantically silhouetted in the dust that all the cars and people had created!

When our tent arrived, it was more of a mini circus tent! It was a dullish green in color and sat stranded, alone and forlorn, on the corner of our land. No sign of sunset or revival dust, just a green tent on damp green grass.

When I drove up and saw it sitting there, I must admit I did quietly laugh out loud (if that's remotely possible). I am smiling as I reminisce, because our revival tent was also a little bit special: A circle of elephants—trunk to tail, trunk to tail, trunk to tail—gaily adorned the inside, which tragically created no end of amusement for those of us easily amused. So when we decided to get a tent for Colour, I was quite adamant to the team that we weren't aiming for the special green version. Having said all that, we did have some memorable meetings in that revival tent as the wee elephants watched on.

Capacity

Our Colour tent arrived and it was actually pretty amazing. It allowed these extra thousand women to attend—and all the despairing females rejoiced!

It was white (hallelujah!) and it had a floor, unlike the elephant version. Air ventilation was completely pathetic, but we rejoiced that we could attend a conference and lose ten pounds in perspiration (bonus!). We ran Colour THREE (1999) with two meetings happening simultaneously, and that year was marked with our new Hub Auditorium and our first-ever marquee packed with beautiful,

amazing, and hungry delegates. There were two worship and support teams, and with our lovely guest speakers and my ever-willing
friends who help carry the platform, we ran madly between the two
locations.

Again, I share these stories because we can easily forget that
everything has a beginning and everything starts somewhere—and
it's in these beginnings that capacity as individuals and capacity
as a team are stretched and grown, stretched and grown, stretched
and grown.

Sometimes people want the end result without the glorious pro-
cesses that come with the territory. So many lessons are learned
along the way, because the end result isn't actually the only result
that God is looking for. The miracle of a journey embarked upon
is in what we experience along the way—the highs, the lows, the
conversations on stairways, the surprises, and the mad crazy miracles are what make it so powerful, exciting, and memorable.

When I look back with affection on that hallway conversation
with Brian, I am so grateful for a husband who believes in me.

He and the men in our church (the elders, board, team, and
the wonderful men in our congregation) have supported us the
entire way. For them also it has been an awakening, but I have to
say that they have truly trusted and believed that what was in our
hearts to achieve was from the Lord. Whenever we turned into
"overwhelmed females" or became a little daunted at the mammoth logistics of venue and operations, they have always lent their
strength and fabulous male perspective.

Alongside for a Reason

As men and women in the Kingdom of God, we are alongside
one another for a reason. We each bring strength and gifting to
the table, and over the coming years we would discover this in

more ways than one. Our combined gifting would not only solve logistical and budget issues, it would also facilitate the rescue and redemption of precious souls around the world. The combination of the caring, maternal heart of women and the "let's make it happen" strengths of the men would become a formidable force.

What was happening in this greater Sisterhood story is that women's ministry was moving from left-of-center in the church list of priorities to main page. This Colour conference and all it represented was about to become one of the major events in our Hillsong calendar, and therefore it was going to require a different level of appreciation, cooperation, and support from everyone.

I'd like to say that every person on our team, both male and female, understood quickly what was within my heart. But as with everything, it was a journey of discovery. However, I will say that I deeply honor my husband for trusting me. When many pastors and leaders were still unsure and reluctant to recognize the potential in women and release them to involvement and leadership within church life, my husband Brian held neither doubt nor prejudice and was empowering women in just about every area of leadership and involvement. If you understand the fivefold ministry principle of *apostle, prophet, evangelist, pastor, teacher* spoken of in Ephesians 4:11, then we as a church had women contributing at every one of these levels. And it is because of this that I believe God's favor has overshadowed and blessed not only our own church, but also our nation.

Hillsong is blessed for many reasons, and if you were to ask Brian why, he will always say it is because of the grace of God. I wrote a book a number of years ago called *Heaven Is in This House*—it gives expression to the heart and soul of our church and the favor and blessing that we have been entrusted and graced with. I strongly believe that one of the reasons why our church draws forth this blessing and favor is because she believes in her daughters.

God clearly believes in women, and the creation moment in

Genesis leaves no doubt that His intent is for "His girls" to come alongside the menfolk and for them to achieve greatness and dominion together. Since this is the case, how frustrating and heartbreaking it must be to the Father to have watched His daughters over the centuries being disregarded, dismissed, and ignored. God knows the depth and potential He has put within the feminine heart, and the contributions we bring to the table as women enable His beloved church (and therefore society) to become all she was originally destined to be.

A Complete Bride

For many years I have said that "Jesus is not coming back for half a bride." The glorious Son of God is coming back for a complete bride—men, women, youth, and children together.

For too many centuries across the historic landscape of the broad and diverse church, women have been sidelined. At times, I'm sure this has been unintentional, because of genuine ignorance or naivety concerning what God actually says about His daughters. At times, cultural and theological beliefs regarding womanhood have passed down through the generations and the daughters have been overlooked or relegated to what is secondary or less. And of course the selfish and sinful nature of mankind can be harmfully dismissive on many levels. However, I believe that the prevailing cause has been a spiritual enemy who since the beginning of time has sought to oppress, contain, and ultimately destroy what is within the feminine heart.

Reclaiming What Was Lost

The funny marquee tent where we all sweltered in the heat, listened intently, and sang our little hearts out—while on a lopsided tilt because (as I mentioned earlier) our landscape volunteers hadn't exactly managed to level the land—became the stage for a crazy moment that sits in my memory as profoundly pivotal. Life is to be enjoyed and appreciated, but lest we ever forget, we are also here to make spiritual darkness tremble and to reclaim what has been stolen from the lives of people.

As we all stood one evening in that hot sticky tent, I remember inviting all who were serious about making a difference in the world to look heavenward with me, and then to dare an unseen spiritual realm to pay attention to what was about to happen.

I had just preached from the revelation of the Micah verses about "gathering the daughters in troops" when suddenly a spirit of militant godly defiance rose within me. As the girls leaned into the almost tangible sense of His presence that had permeated the room and the atmosphere of the Hub Auditorium, I leaned into my King and then followed a leading to commission this company of girls to "dare the enemy to take note of their name because they were about to become his worst nightmare." They were about to challenge his relentless onslaught against the daughters of planet Earth. What ensued was a loud, profound, and sobering moment as two and a half thousand women raised their voices in praise to God and assault to a spiritual enemy. It was a moment that I believe penetrated the heavens and sealed the warrior, warlike aspect of this host of women.

The Sisterhood was truly birthed—she was finding her voice, her stance, and her authority—and history's pages were about to quietly start recording the effect of her individual and collective imprint and presence in this everyday world. Her passion to see God's love prevail in the lives of others was beginning to heighten, and a vision to bring solution to all that was wrong and unjust in the world was intensifying.

God was about to turn up the volume on what had been a whisper.

In the not-too-distant future, that whisper would become a powerful shout! As a gathered—and still gathering—host of women, we were about to discover keys to the kingdom that would heal the brokenhearted, unlock captive doors, and bring freedom and hope to countless thousands waiting in the future. Isaiah 61 was about to be etched into the very fabric and canvas of this rising Sisterhood.

The Spirit of the Lord God is upon me, because the Lord has anointed and qualified me to preach the Gospel of good tidings to the meek, the poor, and afflicted; He has sent me to bind up and heal the brokenhearted, to proclaim liberty to the [physical and spiritual] captives and the opening of the prison and of the eyes to those who are bound,

To proclaim the acceptable year of the Lord [the year of His favor] and the day of vengeance of our God, to comfort all who mourn,

To grant [consolation and joy] to those who mourn in Zion—to give them an ornament (a garland or diadem) of beauty instead of ashes, the oil of joy instead of mourning, the garment [expressive] of praise instead of a heavy, burdened, and failing spirit—that they may be called oaks of righteousness [lofty, strong, and magnificent, distinguished for uprightness, justice, and right standing with God], the planting of the Lord, that He may be glorified...

For I, the Lord, love justice; I hate robbery and wrong with violence or a burnt offering. And I will faithfully give them their recompense in truth, and I will make an everlasting covenant or league with them.

And their offspring shall be known among the nations and their descendants among the peoples. All who see them [in their prosperity] will recognize and acknowledge that they are the people whom the Lord has blessed.

I will greatly rejoice in the Lord, my soul will exult in my God; for He has clothed me with the garments of salvation, He has covered me with the robe of righteousness, as a bridegroom decks himself with a garland, and as a bride adorns herself with her jewels.

For as [surely as] the earth brings forth its shoots, **and as a garden causes what is sown in it to spring forth**, so [surely] the Lord God will cause rightness and justice and praise to spring forth before all the nations [through the self-fulfilling power of His word]. (Isaiah 61:1–3, 8–11 AMP, emphasis mine)

The Wonder Years

The bride was awakening and a magnificent garden was in fabulous preparation, and as the Scripture above says, "rightness and justice and praise" were about to spring forth before the nations with greater intention and intensity.

The wonder years were definitely on the horizon, and our fledgling first steps had taught us an array of first lessons. We had stepped up, stepped out, and stretched, knowing that a new day was dawning. We were realizing with greater clarity that we were clothed in stunning "garments of salvation" (Isa. 61:10) and that we had a message worthy of being shouted from the rooftop.

The psalmist penned, "the world's a huge stockpile of GOD-wonders and God-thoughts" and "I'm thanking you, GOD, from a full heart, I'm writing a book on your wonders" (Psalm 40:4 and 9:1 MSG). Victorian poet Elizabeth Barrett Browning captured the same truth beautifully when she said, "Earth's crammed with heaven." Indeed, Earth is crammed with heaven and the immense stockpile of wealth, wisdom, and destiny sitting within the daughters was about to be watered and nurtured into full bloom. Turn the page with me and allow me to journey with you through some moments and truths that would prove defining for the many who were feeling the tug of God's calling and the excitement of what He was laying before us.

PART TWO

. . .

The Wonder Years

eight

THE WONDER YEARS

(The Language)

I t was late at night and she was a lovely lady from the country.

The conference venue was being reset for the next morning and I was in the parking lot after what had been a full and fabulous day. As I approached my car, a woman emerged from the shadows and rather tentatively said, "Pastor Bobbie, I need to tell you something." I turned to engage this woman, and she said, "I need to tell you that I have never in my entire life had such beautiful words spoken over my life."

The raw reality within that moment remains with me to this day.

A lot of words are spoken at a women's conference. This was back in the day, when great amusement was had over the fact that women apparently speak a staggering 25,000 words a day, compared to a mere 12,000 spoken by the menfolk—perhaps the poor darlings would get more words in if we gave them half a chance! However, jokes aside, when this dear country soul in her mid-age said this to me, a quiet sadness filled my heart.

The timing of all this was the beginning of what I'm going to call "the wonder years of Colour"—years that framed the all-important why and how of things. We had cut the ground, we had taken our first steps, and now we were stepping out in faith on so many levels. Momentum was beginning to be felt, there was excitement in the air, vision was on the table, and women were beginning to find themselves in ways that possibly only heaven will truly give account of. As I write this Sisterhood story, I can see how these next few years of Colour created the foundations upon which God would build. The language within this environment and the words being woven into the fabric of it all were about to prove both critical and defining.

Healing Words

So here we were—a slightly younger city girl (me) and a slightly older country sister, standing under the stars on a balmy evening.

As I recall the conversation, it wasn't the great teaching or preaching that she had heard that day that had caused her to wait for me in the parking lot; it was that when I spoke or addressed the women, I used endearing language such as "sweetheart" and "gorgeous girl."

To me, these words or phrases are completely natural. This is how I speak to my own family, it's how I often relate to friends and loved ones, and although I don't always address our congregations with these exact words, I do relate to them with language that is always laced with affection and warmth. However, when this lovely woman said what she said, it drove home the reality that so many precious people live without love, belief, and the simple affection that words such as these contain

The Sisterhood God-whisper was directed at women who needed to hear that not only did God profoundly believe in them, but so also did a myriad of others. That day I was to be the voice in the crowd who spoke life and belief into a soul parched of affirmation.

In many ways, it should be enough for the human soul to know that God believes in them. However, at the risk of sounding contradictory, it is *not enough*. God never intended His beloved creation to exist without relationship, and especially relationship that affirms personhood and value. As human beings, we are created for family, and while family isn't always perfect, healthy family will always seek to speak words of life over one another and fill the deficit within the human heart that craves belief.

Rise Up, Honey

In that parking-lot moment, God confirmed within me the power within the whisper and that if we were to fulfill the vision and potential of the Sisterhood, we had to tend to the human soul first. The dynamic and influential woman of God (who I believe is within every individual woman regardless of age, status, or history) isn't likely to stand up and change her world if she herself is unable to emerge from her own sadness, despondency, brokenness, or pain.

"Placing value upon womanhood" was the tagline that adorned our early invitations, and it was proving poignantly real in people's lives. In the days ahead, this value would penetrate darkness, challenge injustice, and be felt in communities and nations we were not yet prepared to imagine—but none of this would happen before we had created an environment that would help mend the pain within the sweethearts who were gathering.

If you recall, Cathy Lechner had prophesied, "The women who are crying, I'll give miracles to get them here." The heavens were about to open and unleash miracles with the intent to gather those who were outwardly (or inwardly) crying and beckon them to an environment bathed in Christ's healing presence.

The Spirit of God had a strategic agenda for this strategic gathering of the daughters. He knew what He wanted to accomplish in the days that lay ahead and in the places where this Sisterhood would spread. From where He sat, He could see the end fruit of women rising up to be the voice of hope for others—but He also knew that before that would happen, there were certain tender areas within personal lives that needed attention. A supernatural anointing began to soothe, heal, inspire, and reinstate. I don't know how many letters, cards, and e-mails I received in those early years that said words to this effect: "Bobbie, I was in my seat... and God completely met me where I was at." He met them in their seat and He met them at the various and critical crossroads of their lives.

No One Is Lost in the Crowd

In retrospect, He had to meet them in their seat because there was literally no room for traditional ministry time down the front of the venue. Accommodating the volume of women attending meant that seating pretty much consumed every square inch of carpet, and those on the front row were practically sitting under the nose of whoever was speaking.

But from these early days I learned to encourage women that no one is ever lost in the crowd. They may have come to Colour with the weight of the world on their shoulders or feeling such despair that they could barely breathe. They may have walked in feeling like they could go no further—and yet, again and again, we would hear testimony that God miraculously met them in their seat as they leaned into the worship, the encouragement, and the atmosphere of belief. And of course, the greatest dynamic bringing change was the life-changing Word of God being spoken over and into their lives. The language of heaven, written and spoken, will soothe and heal like no other.

The wonder years were full of crazy, fun, hilarious, and

heart-moving moments. Women are women, and when you lift the ceiling on them, it's amazing what hilarity surfaces—but the greatest wonder was what God was miraculously doing in His daughters.

Midnight Lyrics

I remember a few years into this period speaking at another women's conference in the United States and deciding to take one of the creative videos that I had used that same year at Colour.

As background, I'd been on my treadmill late one evening about ten days out from the Sydney conference. If you've ever organized an event of this magnitude, you'll know that no end of labor goes into its preparation, and sometimes the only time left to replenish body and soul is late at night. Lost in my own thoughts and trying to work up a marginal sweat, I had Bono of U2 fame blaring in my ears, when suddenly an idea spun off one of U2's songs, "Grace." The lyrics of this song perfectly capture the idea that grace finds beauty in everything, and that both goodness and healing can be found within the context of grace.

I jumped off the treadmill, grabbed a scrap of paper, and quickly mapped out what I perceived the creative moment could look like and, more importantly, what it might accomplish in the hearts of the girls it would be for. It may have been after midnight, but you learn to act in the moment. I quickly e-mailed our ever-willing creative team to see if they could produce this idea in the short amount of time available.

I don't know if you know or remember the song, but as I walked and hit the repeat button again and again, it was as though I could see and feel the feminine heart that so often experiences the friction of life and yet selflessly offers grace in its place.

The team were, of course, willing, and what emerged a few days later was a beautiful video presentation of song and image built around the emotive lyrics of the Paul Hewson (Bono) song "Grace." And then the moment that it was truly about: A handful of men addressed the women and sought to place value upon those gathered, from the stance of men, fathers, brothers, and sons.

Robert brought affirmation of value.

Kevin spoke from the stance of a husband and father.

Joel (my then twenty-year-old son) shared from the stance of a young man.

And Josh from the position of a son.

All were gracious and kind and spoke in a manner that acknowledged that sometimes the brothers inflict pain they shouldn't. They gently apologized on behalf of any who may have done so.

It was a sensitive concept, but it was something I honestly felt God's Spirit had prompted me to undertake. When I showed the video in the morning session of Colour, you could feel the effect it was having on hearts watching and listening. I know God did a quiet and deep healing work in those who had been disappointed, hurt, or damaged by the men in their world. I knew also that when I took this same creative piece to Oklahoma, God would use it there—but I wasn't prepared for the conversation that followed.

A woman approached me after the Oklahoma meeting in a similar way to my Aussie sister in the parking lot. She also was a lovely country girl. This is what she said: "Bobbie, I don't know what happened tonight...I've possibly been on three hundred altar calls to get over the pain of my life...but tonight as I watched that video...those men spoke to *me*...Bobbie, they spoke to *me*...and something broke in my life...I feel completely set free!"

As we engaged in conversation, she told me her story.

Her husband had left her for another. He hadn't left her for another woman—he had left her for a man. The personal rejection had completely disabled her ability to move forward. She had obviously gone again and again to the foot of the cross, and she seemed to understand God's personal love and compassion toward her, yet she needed the sense of affirmation that came across in that video. The men in the creative presentation affirmed her value as a woman after her personal value as a woman had been deeply damaged by the most important man in her world. As a handful of the faithful and tender men in my world simply acknowledged the heartache that is too often inflicted by those who should know better (who should love, honor, cherish, and sustain us), this lady remarkably found her freedom.

Healing in His Touch

I don't write this in a manner to shame men or point the finger. We are all sinners in need of salvation, and as much as men can hurt women, women can also hurt men. But the reality remains: There are countless women silently drowning in the pain of their experience—and God knows. He hears the cry of our hearts, and as the Bible says, His hand is "not so short that it cannot save" (Isa. 59:1 NASB). He has a plan of rescue that miraculously involves you and me. God is our Father and we are His kids—and as brothers and sisters doing life together, we can either contribute to the pain or stand and be advocates of value and healing. Heaven believes in us and there is a mandate for us to believe in one another. Such was the heightened revelation rising within this emerging Sisterhood.

The moment in the parking lot in Sydney and the similar moment in Oklahoma confirmed in my own heart the many layers of what would become "the Colour experience." Laughter and lunacy coupled with heaven-breathed moments would mark these wonder years and create whatever was needed to refresh the soul and empower women to move forward in calling and destiny. As the Bible so perfectly puts it, there is healing in His wings: "But to you who fear My name, the Sun of Righteousness shall arise with healing in His wings" (Mal. 4:2 NKJV).

When Jesus walked the earth, healing was found in His approach and touch. The question I present is: What healing will be within our approach and touch as His commissioned, empowered, and anointed daughters? If the mere shadow of ancient disciples like Peter could bring healing and well-being to those in need (see Acts 5), then why not through us also?

Ours Will Become Theirs

Like magnificent storm clouds gathering on the horizon, a great host of women were gathering who would carry words of hope and healing. What was on their lives was about to water the earth and water those in need of good news. Again, the "self-fulfilling power of His word" (Isa. 61:11 AMP) finding residence in us would spring forth like a garden upon the earth, causing rightness, justice, and praise also to spring forth.

The individual and collective testimony of our healing would become their healing. The individual and collective stories of breakthrough and miraculous possibility would become their breakthrough and inspiration. It would be felt as we gathered each year at Colour, and it would be felt as women took the spirit of empathy and true Sisterhood back to their respective neighborhoods, communities, nations, and continents.

Our humble desire is that we would carry the magnificent and all-encompassing grace of our God like a crown upon our head—for all to see.

nine

CHANDELIERS AND CONFETTI

(The Preparation)

*M*um, *women are walking into the auditorium and bursting into tears!"*

I am a romantic at heart and atmosphere is important.

A number of years ago we had a leadership night at church and afterward Brian invited some friends back to our home for coffee. We'd gone in separate cars and somehow they all arrived at the house before I did. I walked into the living room to find this handful of dear friends happily relaxed and settled in after a long but great day. Without saying anything and perhaps not even fully realizing what I was doing, I walked around the room. I switched off the bright ceiling lights and turned on the lamps. I lit some candles and got the fireplace happening. Apparently I had a little audience quietly watching, and then one of the guys said, "Oh, *now* it feels like your house, Bobbie."

Brian is brilliant—he makes life happen; he is the king of spontaneous and the invitation was his idea—but what the room needed was a woman's touch. It's often the same in church life and the house of God.

We're all different and there are always going to be exceptions, but most women have something within that wants to create a sense of warmth, welcome, and expectation when people visit. When I host people in my home (and for the record I am definitely not Martha Stewart), I want them to know they're special and deserving of effort and preparation. Of course, when people pop in unannounced, reception should still be the same, regardless of how empty the fridge or how chaotic the house. I believe there's a principle here that shows us something of God's heart toward us.

He Went to Prepare

In the days leading to his crucifixion, Jesus told his disciples that He was going away to prepare a home for them. He had come from heaven to Earth and was about to fulfill on the cross His mission in coming. He was steeling their hearts for what lay ahead and was making it abundantly clear that God's love for them was so immense that preparation was already under way in heaven (see John 14). I don't know about you, but that thought blows my mind.

I passionately believe that when we also prepare and when we make an effort for others, it tells a story and places value upon them. So back to my son Ben's comment at the beginning of this chapter about a certain reaction as the conference doors opened: "*Mum*, women are walking into the auditorium and bursting into tears!"

There were a number of elements contributing to the emotion being felt that evening, but mostly it was because of a beautiful chandelier hanging from what was our Hills campus ceiling. This particular auditorium officially seats three and a half thousand— more if you pack the floor tight. It is an enormous space to decorate and was built to convention-center standards, so in reality it is a small stadium. That year we wanted to create a living-room feel and an atmosphere of romance for the women gathering.

So, without being asked, a team of fabulous volunteers had

painstakingly strung thousands and thousands of crystals together and created (on a shoestring budget) the most beautiful, giant chandelier, which hung in the center of the room. Complementing the spectacle were dozens of clear lightbulbs hanging off long extension cords with white angel wings attached—an idea I borrowed from a restaurant in Europe. When the doors finally opened and the patiently waiting women started flooding into this awaiting and wonderful atmosphere they could not believe their eyes. So many couldn't fathom that this much effort had been made for *them*! The lights were dimmed; there was majestic emotive music playing. Individual welcome bags were meticulously and perfectly balanced on what was to be their seat. The ambience was as perfect as we knew how to make it, and what was encountered reduced many to tears.

I'm sure there were some who noticed absolutely nothing (God bless them), but for those who did, the moment was divine and told a story. It told them that they were expected, loved, and welcomed. It told them that they were indeed important and worthy of preparation. And it revealed that the effort expended echoed truth from the far reaches of eternity that there is a place prepared for them, and that heaven is always waiting to romance their hearts.

And, unbeknownst to most, every seat in every section of that vast room had also been tenderly prayed over by those entrusted to host those areas. What the girls were experiencing was a tiny taste of heaven's heart toward them.

His Living Room

The Colour experience is about creating an environment where God (and God alone) can move among those gathered.

Shall I say that again? The true spirit of this message—and the events that serve this message—is not about us or anyone else.

It's not about showcasing what we have to offer in gift, talent, or creativity. It's about creating an environment where the King of heaven can easily move among His beloved. Despite the fact that God can actually move in any context, we are also instructed to "prepare the way" for Him—and there is just something about a prepared environment that welcomes the human heart like none other (see Isa. 40:3 and Matt. 3:3).

Psalm 45:11 in the Message says, "Be here—*the king is wild for you*" (emphasis mine). Our responsibility is to help create the "be here" environment in order that God can come and do as He wills. Psalm 45 is a magnificent signature to our story (and I will write of it more in chapters to come), but inasmuch as Colour is about us loving and worshipping the Lord Jesus Christ, it is also about this same Jesus loving and romancing us.

The King is wild for you—and there is nothing inappropriate in this imagery. The Jesus we speak of is the supreme lover of every human soul who has ever walked this earth. He is the pure and majestic darling Prince of Heaven, the bright Morning Star spoken of in Revelation and the One who bottles our every shed tear. He is the Bridegroom for whom all heaven and Earth wait, and the One who will one day return for those who love and long for Him. He's the "wild One"—the King who laid aside divinity and came riding to our rescue—the wild One who gave all because Father, Son, and Spirit would not forfeit nor abandon their love for us.

When God spoke to my heart about creating a conference for women, I had no idea that part of the mandate would entail romancing His daughters in the Love Affair of all love affairs. I had no idea that offering a single red rose at the close of some of our earlier conferences in London and Kiev would reduce many to tears because they'd never been given a rose or flower in their entire life.

I had no idea that training our volunteers with simple kindness, politeness, and thoughtfulness would minister life. I recall a young student volunteer telling how he saw a woman drop something in the busy foyer. He ran after her to hand it back, and when he did, she turned and said, "Young man...no man has ever helped me like this."

I had no idea that the little girl within will always be the little girl within. It doesn't matter what age she is; it doesn't matter how feminine or tomboy she is; it doesn't matter what her profession or calling is; it doesn't matter if she has been badly treated or beautifully loved; it doesn't matter if she thinks she's too cool or whatever for all this romantic talk—that little girl and daughter within needs to be loved, and loved tenderly.

I had no idea that so many women have seldom or never been affirmed, romanced, or prepared for in this manner—and that it was of disturbing concern to the Father. Jesus Christ came to be the tender love of our lives, and the truth of that was being felt.

At the end of the day, chandeliers are chandeliers. They're simply lights made of crystal and glass, but for many there's something about a beautiful chandelier that lifts the human soul from the normality of life to someplace else. Tiaras and crowns, chandeliers and swords began to lift the imagination of this growing Sisterhood into a new realm of reality and authority—an authority that would, in time, redefine harsh realities into something more lovely and beautiful.

Light and Shade of Whatever It Takes

Light and shade became the norm within the wonder years. One minute we were experiencing gorgeous moments inspired through worship and creativity, and the next minute, ridiculous moments had us laughing so hard that tears would roll down our faces. But in the midst of it all, miracles were unfolding. If chandeliers did it for some, then crazy colorful paper did it for others.

Yes, who could imagine that volumes of colorful confetti shot from giant paper guns would create such fun and healing—but it did! In fact, it became a catalyst of healing for someone very close to me.

My own sister-in-law had come to one of the conferences. She's a beautiful woman now in her mid-sixties—talented and kindhearted on so many levels, but life had proven personally disappointing in one or two areas and she was facing her own giants. She hadn't been in the habit of coming to Colour, but one year the sudden passing of a young man in our church had brought her to Sydney for the funeral. The only morning available to celebrate his life was between the two back-to-back conferences that year.

I remember kissing my sister-in-law at the end of the service. Despite the sadness, it was a beautiful late-summer day. As we chatted, she quietly said that she might like to come to the conference. I nearly fainted on the spot. These were words I'd been waiting to hear for so long.

I quickly responded: "Maureen, if you come to this second conference, it will make this Colour for me." I think there is something within all of us that is so desperate for those dearest to us to experience what we are experiencing. So when she said she wanted to come, it truly was the highlight of the week for me.

That evening, we enthusiastically launched into the second conference of whatever year it was. Maureen was about four rows behind me, safely nestled among friends. As the lights dimmed and the opener began, you could feel the anticipation in the room. And then, as was the case in those early years, the opening creative moment hit its crescendo and BOOM...confetti guns shot oceans and oceans of colorful confetti into the air. An enchanting rain of paper then magically floated down over the entire crowd!

Squeals of delight filled the massive room as our worship team took their cue, welcomed everyone, and encouraged the women to their feet. As music and song, worship and praise poured out of the thousands gathered, a miracle was quietly in motion four rows back.

I've always loved the confetti moments, always loved the magic and insane mess they create, and always labored to make sure we could factor them into the budget—but again, I am always overwhelmed at how "little things" like this bring healing and life to dry and thirsty souls within the crowd. My beloved sister-in-law later told me what that moment meant for her.

It took her back to her childhood and reminded her of the girl within—a girl who had hopes and dreams of what life would be. My sister-in-law has raised a fabulous family and is adored by many, but in that season she was unable to surface from something that had crushed her spirit. Somewhere in the confetti and atmosphere of her first-ever Colour, a healing process began and she found the resolve to believe that she could re-emerge. And re-emerge she did.

Today she's part of our greater world and has a heart to speak into the lives of young women and help them learn life's lessons from all she has experienced. When I told her that I was writing about her, she told me that she had never felt such "childlike joy" as in that moment. I love the heart of God and that He will use whatever it takes to outwork His generous heart toward us.

Of course, like everything, we didn't start with giant confetti guns capable of drowning an entire stadium of girls. We started with a ziplock bag of confetti that a fun-loving Californian brought from home. I'm sure heaven smiled to see her teach the Word and then sprinkle handfuls of confetti over whoever was within her reach, to show them that in Christ we are part of a victory parade (see 1 Cor. 15:57). Of course, if you think about it, He actually paints the heavens with color and wonder every single day—from sunrise to sunset, majestic skylines remind us of His presence—yet how many of us busily going about our everyday lives truly have eyes to stop and see it?

More Than a Party

Pages and pages could be written about all the fun and games and crazy challenges that go with throwing a party for thousands of women. From the outset, rolling out the red-carpet welcome became part of who we were—and of course, a party isn't a party without food and gifts (and the odd fireworks display). Regardless of whether you are hosting that party for five beloved girlfriends or thirty-five thousand beloved girlfriends, food and gifts have to be part of the landscape.

God knew the areas of injustice that we would engage in the days ahead. He knew the forgotten and lost people who awaited our arrival and rescue, but He also knew He had work to do first among those early gatherings in Sydney. He knew that hearts needed to be healed and strengthened and that many needed to rise up before they could move forward and move out.

He knew that the beautiful daughters gathering at the beautiful venues in Sydney (venues adorned with chandeliers and confetti) were as important and as in need of tenderness as those awaiting us in less beautiful and less delightful foreign and faraway fields.

He was about to teach us the extreme diversity of placing value upon others—diversity that would at times entail massive innovation, energy, fundraising, and involvement, or diversity that at times would be as simple and understated as an ice cream on a stick or an inexpensive makeup accessory.

With each turn of the page we were prepared for the lesson it held.

ten

TWO-DOLLAR MIRRORS

(The Little Things)

There probably isn't a mom on the earth who hasn't at some point found her little girl prancing or preening in front of a mirror. Even little boys have been known to flex their muscles and find fascination in what looks back at them. A mirror by definition is simply something that gives a faithful reflection, a true picture of something else—although we all know that fitting-room mirrors in any swimwear department are *not* faithful and are part of a conspiracy to destroy all summer self-esteem.

Jokes aside, it was during one of the afternoon breaks at Colour that I encountered the story of a woman whose association with a mirror would tell a story worthy of being retold—a story both heart wrenching and amazing.

Time-Out

In the midst of the intensity (and fun) of conference, creating a little space where you can kick off your shoes and relax for a moment is important. Our time together is compressed into a fast and furious forty-eight hours, and I've learned that a little time-out is needful for *everyone*. Those teaching and carrying the weight of the event need space to breathe and refocus, and those listening need space to process all they are receiving—so somewhere for the delegates to relax in the afternoon is as important as the greenroom space I create for my keynote guests. For all the girlfriends who couldn't nip home for a nap or go back to their hotel for a quick shower, we created some areas to unwind.

• Girls could stretch out on giant cushions on the grass and soak up a little Aussie sunshine—perfect while temperatures didn't soar and grass wasn't reduced to dust, and perfect until someone (hello) decided the cushions must be free and they mysteriously went missing!

• Or they could snuggle up for an afternoon chick flick in the auditorium—always well censored and always a feel-good movie—because being inspired to change the world is emotionally stretching and a little laughter and normality will always help the heart process.

• Those in need of retail therapy (and what woman doesn't feel the need for retail therapy?) could jump on the bus and shop the afternoon away at the local mall.

• Or women could simply wander around the Expo areas at their own pace. The Expo would in later years become the exciting Sisterhood Zone, where hundreds would sign up with friends to "Be the Change" for those in need of help or rescue.

It was as one of my own team wandered through the Expo that she came across the story that she was so keen to share with me that afternoon. As she milled around the various stands, she noticed a woman who was quietly overwhelmed by something. I don't think she was trying to be noticed, I don't think she was trying to make a scene or a fuss, but someone *had* noticed and they weren't about to ignore her emotion.

We labor to instill into the hundreds of volunteers who serve each year at Conference that we are here to assist and complement whatever God is trying to do. This applies to those who teach or lead worship and goes right through to those who clean the bathrooms or keep the traffic flowing. So if someone is distressed or lost or in need of some tender loving care, then by all means (please, please, please) stop, step in, and be of assistance. As I recall, the somewhat distressed woman said to my friend that she had been in the morning session, had loved all that had happened, and had with several thousand other women graciously received her "little gift."

For perspective, each year we give the girls attending a little gift that becomes a memory of our time together. I'm not aware of exactly where or when she opened it—perhaps in her seat or perhaps afterward—but when she did, she was overcome with emotion. The Colour gift that year was a little silver compact makeup mirror. Of course it wasn't really silver but it was cute, and engraved on the tiny mirror inside were the words BEAUTIFUL DAUGHTER— the intent being that every time it was opened, the girls would be met with a few words to give encouragement and make us all smile.

Shattered Image

As this dear woman opened her gift and read those two words now inscribed over her own reflection in the mirror, it was like time stood still as she encountered truth. It was as though her Heavenly Father spoke directly to her daughter heart, and for the first time in her entire life she heard and *believed* that she was indeed beautiful.

As my friend inquired further, this lady opened up and told her that when she was a little girl, her father would grab her by the neck, push her face violently into the mirror, and tell her how ugly she was! My friend was reduced to a deep and sad silence.

I don't know what incites a parent to behave like this. Brian and I have been pastoring long enough to know that hurt people can sometimes lash out and hurt others. This is definitely not true of everyone who has suffered at the hand of another, but internal conflict will often unleash itself on the innocent and unprotected. Unless such issues are dealt with, brokenness will invariably pass from one generation to the next, often strengthening in aggression. I'm sure this is what the Bible is referring to when it speaks of gen-erational curse (see Exod. 20:5, Num. 14:18, and Deut. 5:9). The good news, however, is that people can break curse-like patterns, and one of my all-time favorite messages by my husband was where he declared many years ago to a young and growing congregation that "in Christ" the brokenness can stop with us. We can decide that patterns of anger, violence, aimlessness, depression, alcohol-ism, divorce, or whatever else may have plagued our families for perhaps decades can *end* with us. In our own strength these things may seem impossible, but with God "all things are possible" (Matt. 19:26).

Who knows what would make a father do this to his little girl— a little girl who should be celebrated and treated with tenderness; a little girl who should be told every day that she is beautiful; a little girl whose worth should be cherished and protected, not crushed by such a mindless and selfish act of violence.

I don't know the full complexity of this woman's story—all I know is that one of my beloved girls had encountered yet another miracle in motion, and this is how it was shared with me. Had my friend not walked through the Expo that afternoon, had she not noticed this precious woman, had she not inquired, then I would not be sharing this story with you today. If the lady in question is reading this, I hope that I have recounted this moment as it was.

All I know is that God used an inexpensive two-dollar compact mirror, which has probably been discarded now by most of us, to let you know that you are indeed beautiful in His eyes.

It breaks the Father's heart to see any son or daughter crushed by life, and the Colour story and the Sisterhood message is about restoring that which has been shattered or broken.

Intricate Details

Someone close to you may have spoken soul-destroying words against you, but God always speaks life-giving truth toward you. Someone may have told you again and again that you are stupid or ugly, but as far as God is concerned you are altogether lovely. Someone may have undermined your worth, but heaven valued your worth so much that the Son of God made the ultimate sacrifice for you.

I share this particular story because I am continually amazed at God's providence at work in our lives. He is the God of the entire universe, He spoke the heavens into existence, and yet He is so mindful of the intricate details within our lives. Moments that have wounded or scarred us are private details of our lives that remain critically important to Him, regardless of the passage of time—and given opportunity and occasion, He will move heaven and Earth to orchestrate healing and reverse the damage. This was one such moment. When my friend stood in my backroom area and told me this story, I again felt overwhelmed by His deep love for humanity. Again and again and again, the magnitude of value stolen and value restored was becoming the story of Colour.

When we ordered thousands of inexpensive little mirrors, having decided that they would be that year's Colour gift, I love that God was intently watching from heaven, knowing that one of His precious daughters was about to be set free. I love that He knew she was registered and coming; I love that He knew the exact moment she would receive and open the compact and that He allowed us to inscribe words that would be perfect words of healing for her. I love that even now, many years on, I can revisit this story and hopefully someone else who needs to hear that they are beautiful will allow the words on these pages to be their moment of truth.

Assault on the Future

God is beautiful, and so are you! He is the origin and essence of all goodness and He will go to enormous lengths to restore that goodness back to those from whom it has been stolen. Sometimes it may feel like forever for all the pieces to come together, but if we all allow Jesus access to work in our lives and if we trust Him, He will prove Himself faithful. He is well able to mend and heal, and then use whatever harshness has been perpetrated against you to bring healing to others.

We are living in an age where there is an unprecedented assault against children. Childhood is being undermined and attacked on many sides. Image distortion is sadly no longer the exclusive domain of teenagers and young women. Reports tell of an alarming number of small children being treated for eating disorders and related diseases. A truly disturbing demand for child pornography is fueling a heinous lust and industry against children, and easy access on the Web is magnifying the problem to alarming levels. Even social and economic demands upon young and well-meaning working families are adding pressures that can take their toll.

Childhood is under attack because childhood represents the future. And if childhood can be marred or damaged, then the wonder and beauty of adults who grow into their full stature and God-invested potential is sabotaged.

Satan knows this, and this is why the wonder years of Colour were laying critical foundations of restoration. As important as the Word of God being spoken over our lives were, the little things—little gifts and little gestures we kept stumbling upon—were also being powerfully used by God's Spirit.

They weren't just the party trimmings of a chick conference. They had purpose and meaning, and over the coming years I would discover again and again how critical the gifts and details were. God was seeking to restore lost childhood. He was seeking to restore the stolen years and the years the Bible refers to as devoured by the locusts (see Joel 2:25). He was wanting so many of His precious daughters to sing again as in the days of their youth, when life was perhaps less complicated, complex, or disappointing.

Relentless Love

Beautiful verses are found in the Old Testament book of Hosea. They reveal to us the heart of the Father toward His children, and they are verses that my own heart often goes to when considering and praying for the Sisterhood.

They speak of God's relentless love for His people and how He has the capacity to take our troubled lives and turn them around. It speaks of a "Valley of Trouble" (Hosea 2:15 NLT) being turned into a "door of hope and expectation" (Hosea 2:15 AMP). It speaks also of His ability to heal the human heart and cause it to sing there "and respond as in the days of her youth" (Hosea 2:15 AMP).

We all know that beauty is in the eye of the beholder and that true beauty runs deeper than what is external—however, there isn't a woman or girl alive who hasn't been affected in some way by what is seen or perceived in the reflection of a mirror. Whether we admit it or not, we are fragile beings and the words spoken over our lives are important.

So I love that on this particular year in our Colour journey, a little imitation-silver two-dollar mirror with two little words inscribed within would play such a beautiful role in restoring the dignity of one woman whose worth was important. Two little words of life on our part faithfully reflected an eternal truth that God longs for every woman to hear.

I also love that mirrors would play a role in the restored dignity of women in a faraway land. In 2007, a strategic partnership in Africa would cause us as a global Sisterhood to encounter the lives of war-affected women who had been insanely brutalized in a civil war that had raged against their community and families.

As we leaned into their plight, empathized with their struggle, and sought to give whatever strength we had to their recovery, we would play a humbling role in helping them find the courage to once again look at their reflection and not feel shame for what had been inflicted upon them. Instead of a face bearing witness to cruelly severed lips, nose, or ears, restorative plastic surgery (financed through the Sisterhood) would allow them to once again look in a mirror and encounter a reflection of newness and hope.

The journey of discovering how important the Colour gifts were was well and truly in motion. Candy, confetti, and chocolate-coated ice creams en masse were marking the playful, party aspect of Colour, while mirrors and makeup cases, knitting needles and teapots, freedom shirts and drink bottles would prove just as important and strategic in the greater message of value as the many spiritual moments we were to experience.

Equally important would be the band of amazing friends who would align their hearts and bring what was upon their lives.

The Colour table was becoming a diverse offering of gift and talent, anointing and devotion—a table that would inspire and feed many with vision and hope, a table that we would affectionately refer to as being "set." And one that we would all feel deeply honored and privileged to be a part of.

eleven

COLORFUL THREADS

(The Friendships)

Each friend represents a world in us, a world not born until they arrive, and it is only by this meeting that a new world is born.

ANAÏS NIN

The wonder years of Colour were rich in friendship.

Old friends and new friends alike were being etched into a storybook of friendship that in essence is the true spirit of Sisterhood. As Anaïs Nin profoundly declares, each friendship represented a world, and for us it felt like an ocean of worlds were colliding. These foundational years also felt like tapestry in motion. Tapestry has been described as a heavily woven cloth of rich and varicolored designs; a combination of scenes; a sequence of events; a tapestry of cultures.

Cultures that were geographical in nature, cultures shaped by legacy and experience, and cultures defined by the calling and anointing upon the many lives being knit together were contributing to this rich and many-sided tapestry of friendship that God was masterminding. As the definition also suggests, a combination of scenes and events, families, and personal histories were being woven into something that God had designed, to tell a powerful story of empathy and cohesion and the endless possibilities of unity.

True friendship is uncomplicated. It may not be perfect, but if it is pure in spirit it will allow for the ebb and flow of life.

It's generous, encouraging, and never competitive. It's not easily threatened and leaps to the defense or protection of those to whom it is loyal. It remains faithful in all seasons, is tested with the passage of time, and always finds grace to forgive when forgiveness is needed. It believes the best of one another and is undaunted when distance or busyness of life creates a widening space between that last coffee or shared giggle and the present.

I trust that I have been a loyal friend to all the women I'm about to mention. I know I am personally and eternally grateful for all they have deposited into my life, and I know that I am a stronger and better person for having met and known them. My world expanded when I encountered them, and I know their world expanded when they met us. My prayer is that as we engage the future and continue to scribe this story together, the Father will watch from heaven and smile. I pray that the example we bring to those watching will be pure, Christlike, and honoring in every way.

Eternally Grateful

I named this chapter "Colorful Threads" because the language seemed perfect and appropriate to describe what was taking place—the colorful threads and strands of our collective lives were indeed being woven together into a strand of unity that would draw forth the blessing of God. Psalm 133 says that where there is unity, GOD commands blessing. I am eternally grateful for each and every friendship, and I want to take time to give honor where honor is due.

I'm grateful for a fun-loving Californian. I'm grateful for her sparkle and joy and cute skinny butt (which of course none of us ever envy). I'm grateful that she hasn't missed one Colour in our twenty-year history. She told me years ago that she never would, to which I said: "Babe, never say never"—but I am grateful that she is always there and always kisses my face after I've spoken. Her love language is encouragement, and one of the things she is passionate about is friendship. She has overcome cancer and for this we are grateful.

I'm grateful for a beautiful Canadian. She will probably laugh out loud when she reads this, but she's like Mother Earth—soft, warm, embracive. I often refer to her as a safe place, and I always smile when I see her arrive. Over the years, the anointing that is upon her life with regards to family has healed many and brought hope to countless homes represented by those who have leant into her wisdom.

I'm grateful for a petite blonde. Our worlds collided in the very early years of Colour, and she helped us harness an awareness and concern for young women dealing with the fallout of fractured esteem. I'm grateful for the early years of her involvement, for her passion in the Word, and for her helping us understand more clearly an epidemic of need that sits not far beneath the surface of today's youth. I will always cherish a moment in the car when she leaned forward, holding a certain Colour invitation in her hand (the one with the tiara crowns), and told me it was the most brilliant and impacting thing she had ever seen. The encouragement went deep.

I'm grateful for a passionate Greek. She wandered into our church many years ago as a broken young woman and has emerged with a testimony that is a weapon in her Savior's hand. I'm grateful for her friendship. I'm grateful for her endless "pump-factor" (her enthusiasm). I'm grateful that she refers to Brian and me as her spiritual parents and besties, and despite a global ministry still refers to Sydney as home.

I'm grateful that she understands the spirit and mandate of this movement and has earned a platform around the world to articulate what it is truly about. I'm grateful that we carry this dream for womanhood together and as the Bible says, "two are better than one, because they have a good return for their labor" (Eccles. 4:9). The future of Colour rests in God's hands, and I am grateful that whatever direction the future takes, my friend will constantly be at my side. I also love our shared passion for chocolate-coated licorice bullets and confess that once we start we have been known to devour truckloads together.

An Army of Brilliant Women

I'm grateful for an army of brilliant women within our own Hillsong Church. They are the true armor-bearers, true co-laborers, and true vision carriers! They are the "whatever it takes" women who give heart and soul to carry what is upon our collective lives, calling, and house.

Some could launch out and perhaps build their own ministry platform, yet personal conviction about planting and calling positions them differently. Their example on the ground has enabled many around the world to see and glean from the enormous possibilities that "local Sisterhood within local church" brings to the table.

Some of them carry leadership responsibility and some are entrusted with teaching platforms across our church, but most are the faithful girls who faithfully serve behind the scenes. They are content to be unseen and are seldom in the spotlight, yet any fruit this story is bearing belongs to them.

They are young and old and everything in between. They are wives and moms and grandmothers. They are educators and homemakers, career women and college students. And they are bright, intelligent, and delightfully down-to-earth.

They are the astounding everyday girls who have become the true foundation and building blocks upon whom God has built this message. They've taken whatever God has put in our hand to do, and they've proven faithful to it. Their devotion has given Sisterhood its strength and integrity, and they are the girls who are my first priority.

Whenever I am around them, I feel grounded and safe. They've seen me live and learn the rhythm of this message. They've trusted me and encouraged me every inch of the journey, in season and out of season, when surrounded with blessing or surrounded with challenge, and inasmuch as I am deeply proud of them, I know they also are proud of me. We are connected heart and soul and shoulder to shoulder, and we are doing life together. I love and respect them beyond what words can express.

In the earlier days, these local women I am honoring (and perhaps waxing a little too poetic about) were of course the Aussie-based Hillsong girls, but nowadays our world has expanded into faraway nations and cities, so they are girls from literally all over the world.

In many ways, I am at a loss to know how to show my gratitude for this growing family of sisters and friends. In a lovely way, it seems that God is adding faster than we can count. When we plant new locations and new rooms within our Hillsong vision ("one house, many rooms"), it is as though the spirit of Sisterhood is so anticipated and so welcome that it doesn't take long for the seeds sown to surface, bud, and fruit.

And then there are the truly amazing "others." These are the women who over the years have become true sisters and true comrades in all the wonder, fun, and games. They come from other places and other plantings and are the girls who at different times grace our growing Colour teaching platforms. I deeply love, admire, and trust them. I know that the future has many more amazing women, whom we are yet to encounter in His perfect timing, and I look forward to all that the future holds.

The Real Heroes

I had always known deep within my heart that the greater message of Sisterhood was about the everyday girls and the difference they would make in their local communities. There will always be those who will hold the microphone, grace the teaching platforms, and rally the troops. There will always be those who attract more attention and somehow end up in the limelight—however, the real story is being written and woven by thousands of everyday girls who may never travel the world or ever find themselves in any spotlight, but trust me, they are in the spotlight of heaven and they are the real heroes.

With time, I would learn how to champion these girls and tell some of their stories in a manner that would allow their courage and innovation to be an inspiration to others.

Their willingness to "Be the Change"—in their community, their homes, their workplaces—and their willingness to contribute their equally significant measure and gift would become a fresh benchmark of possibility for the many who sometimes think that their small part is of no significance. Their stories have brought true richness and depth to the tapestry called Colour.

Purity

God had (and has) sown and planted His "daughter troops" in every nation and corner of the earth—they just needed to be faithfully found and mobilized. New worlds and new fields were constantly opening up, and I believe God was gathering and seeking to further commission trustworthy women who would carry the same commission into their neighborhood, wherever that might be. He was looking for women who would understand mandate, appreciate cohesion, value unity, remain faithful, and carry the seeds of this precious message carefully into the regions they call home.

May we never forget that the seeds of this message are indeed precious, because there still remain nations and pockets of humanity who have waited centuries for someone to come with a message of freedom and liberation to all that is feminine. To observe any compromise on this message is something that will always cause me concern. So for the sake of integrity and stewardship, I will say that there have been times when we have quietly grimaced because well-meaning people have come to Colour and completely misunderstood the revelation and misobserved what God has been doing in Australia.

The real message runs so much deeper than hosting a flashy event—the real message is noble and pure! It's way more than big crowds, big venues, stage, and lighting. It's more than fancy creative production and perceived opportunity that comes with the territory. The real message is not a means to an end; it is not about growing one's ministry or church in a pragmatic way; it is definitely not the latest fad to jump onboard with; and it is definitely not a ticket to enter the next or current circuit of conference speakers.

The real message is first and foremost about knowing and loving the Lord Jesus Christ as Lord and Savior. It's about being found—found in His grace and goodness—and a myriad of other wonderful realities that come to life when we realize that Jesus really is the Way, the Truth, and the Life. It is about no-nonsense discipleship that grows you to places of maturity. The gospel is tender but not soft—so also the Colour message. It compels to a higher calling and a higher response.

It is about the Father heart of God for His daughters, and His endless desire for our hearts to be knit with His, bringing blessing and solution to the earth. It is about allowing the Holy Spirit to be the Holy Spirit in our lives—umpire and teacher, the One who reveals all things true, perfect, and correct.

It's about the church being strong and vibrant with a healthy mind-set and attitude toward women and womanhood. It's about allowing the daughters to be front and center of kingdom purpose.

It's not self-seeking but generational, empowering others to rise up and fulfill what is upon their lives. It is about feminine expression finding expression. It is about bringing tangible and felt change in areas of need. And it's about the purity of women, diverse in nature and calling, being united in friendship and cause.

The Colour Conference (and Sisterhood) is *an outflow of an honest commitment to the health and well-being of the women in one's local church, local community, and local planting.* It isn't about Bobbie Houston, fancy speakers, fame, fortune, or opportunity (or anything else that may come to mind). It is about inspiring women to genuinely care about one another, the communities they inhabit, and the overall plight of humanity. It's also about women rising with a healthy and stunning attitude toward church and kingdom cause.

Landscape

Every generation has a landscape to steward and be responsible for. The landscape of the Body of Christ worldwide was changing and so also was the global face of Sisterhood and ministry in and through women. Many would agree that an awakening was happening within the pocket of time that framed these wonder years. I am not so presumptuous as to believe that we were the only players in this awakening—however, God was definitely using the Hillsong Colour environment to either shake or adjust certain mind-sets about women within the greater Body of His church. God has a strategic plan for His church, and unless the foundations are as He would have them, the building He has in mind will not emerge. The Apostle Paul expresses it perfectly to the Ephesians:

> *God is building a home.* He's using us all—irrespective of how we got here—in what he is building. He used the apostles and prophets for the foundation. Now he's using you, fitting you in brick by brick, stone by stone, with Christ Jesus as the cornerstone that holds all the parts together. We see it taking shape day after day—a holy temple built by God, *all of us* built into it, a temple in which God is quite at home. (Ephesians 2:19–22 MSG, emphasis mine)

Regardless of analogy, the colorful threads of our lives were not just being woven so a pretty picture, building, canvas, or story could emerge—there was way more at stake. Women and girls around the world were waiting to hear the message of value and freedom, aching hearts were waiting for relief, and prison doors (figurative and literal) were closer to being unlocked than when we first began.

God was calling, preparing, and positioning His faithful ones to carry the good news—and whatever God was weaving was about to become a weapon of hope in His master plan. I trust your heart is enlarging with each turn of the page, and that you can see yourself and those in your world of influence being woven into this storybook and tapestry of good news.

twelve

FUR BALLS AND KINDNESS

(The Madness and Wonder)

I t was the Year of the Rubber Glove and the Year of the Fur Ball.
It was also 2003. The threat of chemical warfare was strong
in the Middle East, and the SARS virus had travelers packing
surgical masks into their carry-ons. Apple had just launched the
iTunes Store, and unusually high temperatures were being recorded
across Europe. The United States experienced the most daunting
electrical blackout in its history, affecting almost fifty million lives,
and Michael Jackson was in the limelight for behavior not related
to music. *Finding Nemo* (starring Bruce the shark and showcasing
Australia's glorious Barrier Reef) had just been released, and the
star of *The Terminator* had just been elected governor of California.

The world was indeed proving complex and colorful, and I had
a word resonating in my spirit for the girls and the pending Colour
gathering in March. The word was "kindness." Many people can
mistakenly think that God is *not* kind, but contrary to that percep-
tion, the Bible has much to say about the subject.

The Old Testament constantly reveals a God who is gracious and
merciful, slow to anger, and abundant in kindness (see Neh. 9:17).
Countless passages speak of his kindness being our comfort and
strength, and there is one passage that says kindness is one of the

major things he asks from us. Of the famous Proverbs 31 woman, it says that she opens her mouth with wisdom and on her tongue is the law of kindness (see Prov. 31:26). Perhaps the most profound verse that reveals God's insane love is Romans 2:4, where we are told that it is the kindness of God that leads us to repentance. If God (Father, Son, and Holy Spirit) were not kind, flawed humanity would have been abandoned to the wind as a lost cause a long time ago.

Our great forerunner Paul further teaches us that the fruit or evidence of the Spirit in our lives is revealed in kindness—and not only kindness, but love, joy, peace, long-suffering, goodness, temperance, and faithfulness also (see Gal. 5:22). To the church in Ephesus he writes: "In the ages to come he might show the exceeding riches of his grace in *his kindness toward us* in Christ Jesus" (Eph. 2:7 JUB, emphasis mine). I love to think that the ages to come written of here would include us and that we in turn will be advocates of that same kindness into the ages following us. Eugene Peterson's modern paraphrase scribes it like this:

> Now God has us where he wants us, with all the time in this world and the next to shower grace and kindness upon us in Christ Jesus. Saving is all his idea, and all his work. All we do is trust him enough to let him do it. It's God's gift from start to finish! We don't play the major role. If we did, we'd probably go around bragging that we'd done the whole thing! No, we neither make nor save ourselves. God does both the making and saving. He creates each of us by Christ Jesus *to join him in the work he does*, the good work he has gotten ready for us to do, work we had better be doing. (Ephesians 2:7–10 MSG, emphasis mine)

The last sentence in that verse is nothing short of beautiful and challenging. "He creates each of us . . . to *join* him in the work he does"—it represents a glorious invitation, and an invitation that we best be found doing.

Creative Enthusiasm

In my enthusiasm to teach, preach, and drive this fabulous exhortation to kindness home, we decided to create a little visual experience. Our gift that year would be *a set of colorful rubber gloves*. Yep, colorful kitchen gloves—the kind you find under the sink, the kind you slide your hands into in a bid to protect them from the harshness of the work to be done, and the kind that come in an array of colors. I can't fully recall the entire process of reasoning, but in essence it went something like this:

- The world is a mess—our response is intervention!
- If humanity is in trouble, then to the rescue we will come!
- Women are not afraid of mess—a little dirt and drama never deterred any woman on a mission!
- We will roll up our sleeves, step into the fray, and make whatever difference we can!
- Jesus stepped into our mess and surely we can do likewise!
- If He needs us, we will join Him in His work!
- A set of colorful rubber gloves will be the perfect symbolic gift to remind us of our mission and labor!
- The girls can hang them in their kitchen, workplace, or wherever they decide as a reminder of who we are and what we are about!
- Boom! The girls are going to love this!

Little did we know how glorious, wonderful, ridiculous, and fun this idea would be. Team is everything and the team thought this was a genius idea. I love people who never look at you forlornly across the planning table and tell you why something can't be done. I'm sure there have been times when they've left that planning table and wondered, "Is she on drugs or something?" But this was a fun idea that they couldn't wait to get their hands into (excuse the pun).

Hi Ho, Hi Ho, It's Off to Work We Go

Like an army of fairy-tale helpers, off to work they enthusiastically went, rigorously sourcing enough rubber gloves to accommodate the gathering host. These days we would probably go directly to the manufacturer, but who knows where they found seven thousand pairs of gloves that year. There was probably an unusual shortage of kitchen gloves in the outer suburbs of Sydney, as volumes of gloves were mysteriously snapped up from supermarkets everywhere.

And because no one in my world is content to be normal, and because going the extra mile is part of our DNA, and because such moments need to be highly memorable, we decided to glam the gloves with funky fake fur around the edges. The industry of pasting fake fur around the edges of seven thousand pairs of gloves—which if you do the math is fourteen thousand individual gloves—went into motion.

That year, every man, woman, college student, and innocent bystander in our church was commandeered for weeks and weeks and weeks and weeks of fur pasting. Some of this was a little unbeknownst to me, because the team leave me to create the conference in other ways, but I even heard that Pastor Robert Fergusson (one of our lovely pastors and Bible teachers) had his living room turned into one of the many workshops that were scattered across Sydney's northern suburbs. As everyone went to work cutting and pasting, cutting and pasting, cutting and pasting, an insane volume of synthetic fur was apparently inhaled, hence the joke that many were suffering "fur balls" from the mammoth effort being undertaken. However, when the actual moment arrived, it was worth the synthetic discomfort. The things we do for love!

The Big Reveal

The team had laboriously placed each set of gloves inside a budget-saving paper sandwich bag and secured the bag with a wooden clothespin. The bag would keep the gloves a surprise until their moment of reveal.

Day Two of the conference arrived, and I taught what I believe was an important signature message called "Kindness Rules"—and then off the back of the message I said: "Okay, girls, we have a gift for you." The lights went down, the band struck up, the singers and dancers invaded the stage. I left the stage because (hello) singing and dancing isn't my forte. And then, like an army on a mission, hundreds of volunteers emerged from every door in the auditorium. Up and down each aisle they went, passing out thousands and thousands of mysterious brown paper bags.

I will never ever forget watching as an ocean of intrigued women passed each bag along the row and then, when it looked like everyone had one in their hand, they pulled out the colorful gloves! The looks of surprise, wonder, and sheer bewilderment were priceless. Hot pink gloves with a crazy zebra print. Pale green gloves with bright pink leopard spots. Powder-blue ones with insane fluffy white trim—I'm sure anyone who scored the fluffy white ones inhaled enough synthetic fiber to clothe a small village.

And then, without any prompting, seven thousand party-loving chicks donned their somewhat hilariously oversized gloves (size 9! What woman has a size 9 hand?) and started singing and waving along with the madness of the moment. It was the most ridiculous, gorgeous, and fabulous sight ever! As I looked out over this ocean of swinging, swaying, dancing, and then worshipping hands, God opened my eyes yet again to the wonder of an army of women who could change their world if they caught the vision.

I'd seen this army when God originally whispered in my heart—do you remember the stadium moment with Wendy at my side? I'd seen this army in the ancient words of Micah: "Now gather yourself in troops, O daughter of troops." I'd seen this army in the tent, when thousands of girls had raised their voice in defiance against a spiritual enemy. I'd seen it in the meaning of the word "manifold"—the manifold glory and goodness and kindness of God entering the human arena as a force to be reckoned with.

And here we were again, but this time the army was waving an array of colors that represented an array of responses. For me, it sits as one of the most memorable moments ever, although I do have to say that the wonder just keeps getting better and better with each passing year.

Catalyst of Change

The Colour Your World women's conference was now marked with colorful gloves and an even more colorful mandate that, indeed, *Kindness Rules*. If we decided, it could rule in our own hearts and lead us safely. If we decided, it could rule over the despair encountered in others, leading them also to freedom; and if enough of us got on board, it could rule as a powerful catalyst of change helping to relieve many of the pressures facing this world.

Mary of Bethany, whose story we find in the gospels (see Matt. 26:6–13, Mark 14:3–9, and John 12:3–8), was a catalyst of change. She is the Mary who sat worshipfully at Jesus' feet, choosing what was better and more needful in the moment, while her dear sister Martha fussed and busied herself with things that possibly could have waited. Mary had drawn from His presence and tasted of His kindness, and in turn became an agent of kindness. There is nothing idle in true worship. It will infuse the soul and enable us all to enter the fields of calling before us (and engage the everyday activities of our lives) with renewed passion, strength, and understanding.

When Mary broke an expensive vial of ointment over Jesus prior to His crucifixion in a bid to value, love, and anoint Him, her critics harshly rebuked her—but Jesus responded to leave her alone, "...she has just done something wonderfully significant for me" (see Matt. 26:10–13 MSG). She may not have fully understood the magnitude of what was happening, but she understood how precious her Lord was. She responded to His kindness with kindness—and He responded to her gesture of love by proclaiming that what she had just done for Him was profoundly important. Her story of kindness offered and kindness extended would be told again and again down through the corridors of time.

Our kind and loving Savior left the perfection of heaven and did a deeply significant and kind thing for us. He descended into the mess of our lives in a bid to rescue us—and now an army of everyday women was preparing to join Him in His passion and pursuit to walk kindness into the broken and desperate lives of those still in need of His redemptive touch.

Humanitarian Leader

The Church of Jesus Christ has always been about "good works"—or at least it should be. The awakening I have mentioned was happening and within the Body of Christ; our eyes were being lifted to see a broader world in need. What God was doing among His girls in these wonder years was to play a pivotal role in that awakening.

When I look back to that year, 2000, I see it was a signature year in every way. It marked a new chapter in the humanitarian aspect of both the conference and the Sisterhood, and it would point to a coming-of-age that wasn't far off. We had always had a heart to help people. The woman of God spoken of in Proverbs 31 is both *humanitarian* and *leader*. She leads by example in marriage, ministry, and motherhood. She is an entrepreneurial leader, innovative in spirit and style. She is a smart and savvy businesswoman. Within her lies the capacity to faithfully manage "her vineyard" (her family and personal world)—and yet she can lift her eyes and engage the challenge of influencing other fields that are full of need. At the very core of her being is a heart of kindness.

The chapter speaks of her opening her filled hands in a manner that I believe relates to injustice and global need: "She opens her hand to the poor, yes, she reaches out her *filled* hands to the needy [whether in body, mind, or spirit]" (Prov. 31:20 AMP, emphasis mine). The filled and now colorfully adorned hands of thousands of women aligning their hearts with this message of value were beginning to find their human touch.

In all honesty, nothing is new under the sun. God has always had His hands-on laborers; however, the church has never been more empowered to bring change and solutions than she is now. There exists in our personal here and now a planet in desperate need of intervention. It's our planet and those in need are our brothers and sisters. As followers of Christ, as servants and handmaidens, and as His hands and feet, we have a critical part to play in His redemption plan for them.

Somewhere in the mix of these very early wonder years, I remember a friend grabbing me after I had delivered my opening Colour message. It was back in the days of our Hub auditorium, so it really was in the formative years. I had just seeded and added the words "Warrior Princess Daughter" to the greater message.

If I am brutally honest, I was a tiny bit embarrassed by the use of the word "warrior." I know I am a romantic and I know I often express things in a poetic way, but I hate the thought of being cheesy or weird. So to use the word "warrior" in context of the church and this army of women was a little on the edge for me, until a friend shared the following vision that she had had during the worship that very night. Her vision went like this:

> She was standing in a great valley.
>
> The great army of God was gathering and she was observing all that was taking place. Jesus, our Commander in Chief, was at the forefront. My friend recalls that there was movement in this scene, but in her mind it seemed that more should be happening. In the vision she turned to Jesus and said, "Lord, there's movement but not enough."
>
> He looked at her and replied, "I AM WAITING FOR THE WOMEN!"

My friend, who is a respected pastor, nearly died when my message that night confirmed what she had perceived in this vision. She approached me at the end of the night and couldn't hold back the tears. I remember quietly listening amid the bustle and noise of everyone leaving. Over the years, I have held this vision close to my heart, I have allowed it to strengthen me when I needed it, and I have shared it when appropriate with listening ears.

Not Half a Bride

As I said before, Jesus is not coming back for half a bride—He's coming back for a complete bride. He's coming back for a church in full stature and harmony. He's coming back for an army of believers—men, women, and youth alike—who in these latter and final days will effectively beckon a lost and hurting world home.

Without being presumptuous, I can say it was apparent that Colour was playing a strategic role in helping the women gather. Jesus was waiting for the women. He was waiting for His beloved daughters to be recognized and welcomed to front and center of His plan of salvation for the earth.

In some places around the world, recognition of the daughters would jolt thinking and fly in the face of tradition and religion. For those open to His Spirit, it would bring gracious correction and change. And in other places, it would facilitate a simple adjustment in perspective that would unearth a wealth of strength, resource, and gold within the women of some already strong and amazing churches.

It was a pivotal year on a number of fronts. A forty-five-minute sermon about kindness would turn an important page in this Sisterhood story, and an ocean of colorful gloves would mark the beginning of a memorable new era—a new era that would position this maturing Sisterhood amid the seriously hurting, isolated, and forgotten of this world. The kindness of Christ, in and through an army of everyday women, was about to be felt like never before. The troops were gathering, and what we had figuratively been referring to as "an army" was beginning to take literal shape.

Orphans, sisters, and nations were new language about to be scribed into the story—as was a date with a petite Texan who spoke a word that pierced my own heart and caused a response that cannot be omitted from this story.

thirteen

WATERFALLS AND FLAGS

(The Vote)

She was petite, she was blonde, and she was from Texas.

They say that everything about Texas is big and larger than life. Well, she wasn't big, but she packed a punch. One night she paused midsentence, hesitated, and then said the most random thing into the atmosphere. Allow me to walk you into the moment...

The timing was the turn of the millennium (2000 and 2001), and this little lady I want to share about graced our platform for two very important years. What she contributed was like two strokes of color to an already blossoming canvas, adding depth and intrigue to all that was taking shape. One related to the generations, and one related to the nations.

The lopsided marquee tent had moved! It was now located on the other side of the property in the already developed parking lot, and we were hosting not only simultaneous conferences but also back-to-back conferences in a bid to accommodate the flood of women pouring into Sydney. These were the crazy years when our team continued to be an endless source of innovation and delight. For a handful of years, this team I speak of would remove all the new plants and trees from the parking lot gardens so the marquee could be erected, and then replant them when we were done. I need a little raised-eye icon here, because honestly *who does that?!* But where there's a will, there's always a way, and they transplanted native Australian trees till the trees were too big to transplant.

We'd also graduated to a sprung-floor marquee (very posh), and it had real air-conditioning (hallelujah). If the year I'm referring to is correct (smile), then during Week One of conference we sweltered in scorching temperatures (despite the air-conditioning), and in Week Two we almost floated away as the heavens opened and poured torrential rain on our parade (hilarious). However, these were the days when nothing daunted enthusiasm or vision.

Banners and Creative Briefs

Colour was in full motion, and the Colour invitations (and the messages they communicated) were becoming more and more important to the integrity of the story. Brian and I have been blessed with an amazing communications team who understand the devotion and hours that go into any successful campaign designed to carry an important vision and theme. Carefully etching every sentence, word, and image onto the pages became something that consumed my energy for months and something that has become the all-important creative palette and brief of the actual event. If you've ever managed creative minds, you'll understand how important these elements are to enabling talented people to accurately execute what is in your heart. Never assume that they're seeing exactly what you are seeing.

For perspective, the 2000 banner adorning the stage was the gorgeous WARRIOR PRINCESS DAUGHTER one. This was back in the day before we had fabulous digital screens, and I still have one of these banners hanging floor-to-ceiling in my office. Its edges are fraying and it is water-stained from a tropical storm, but I can't bring myself to discard it. One of these days I am going to frame it as a memoir to the beauty and truth within its imagery.

The following year (2001), what hung behind the stage was an equally stunning image of three Aussie girls on an Aussie beach, one of them proudly holding an Australian flag that is billowing wild and free in the ocean breeze and sunshine. It definitely painted a picture that God would use that weekend—and in the midst of all this imagery (I will mention another in a moment) was this little lady from Texas.

Rachel and her husband had hosted youth camps each summer that for many years drew young people (sometimes as many as twenty-five thousand) from all across the United States. She came highly recommended as a seasoned Bible teacher, and I knew that her heart for young people would be perfect for the many young girls gathering now to Colour. The starchy barriers that separated youth and adult had been broken, and it was quite natural for the young ones to want to be there. My own daughter and her young vibrant friends were eagerly in the mix of women gathering.

Freeze Frame

On the Friday evening, as both venues heaved with the energy of all that was happening, I decided to nip over to the marquee where Rachel was about to speak and minister. It was the weekend, so we had opened the flaps, allowing more young girls to squeeze in.

As I sat in the creamy white canvas of this tent, all the young girls had pressed round the edges of the stage and were even on the steps leading up to it. With her gorgeous Southern accent and manner, Rachel had everyone eating out of her hand—and then, somewhere in her message, she just sat down on the edge of the stage and nestled herself affectionately into the middle of all the young girls.

Freeze frame! It was like heaven froze the moment, flicked everything into slow motion, and branded my spirit again. It was the God-whisper tangible, felt, and literally before my eyes..."Create an environment for young women, girded about with older women, and tell them." Here in this summery, steamy marquee setting was the vision (yet again) in stunning motion—an older woman surrounded with young, wide-eyed, and inquiring girls absorbing every morsel of wisdom that fell from her lips.

There are so many layers to Sisterhood. As important as making a difference to the insane challenges facing the world is, so also is making a difference to those nearest to us. *Our daughters and their friends* are in essence our sisters and they are critically important. Sisterhood is about sharing life with them in a manner that is natural and unforced—if you've already raised teenagers or have them, you'll know this is sometimes easier said than done. It's in this natural sharing of life that wisdom is beautifully exchanged.

God is completely generational. The generations matter to Him, and He has designed life to be long and blessed with stories and wisdom, lessons and mistakes, testimony and legacy being passed down through the generations so that each generation can strengthen. Psalm 145 speaks of generations pouring forth the fame of His great name. In all honesty, if we could all get this right, the world would be a better place.

I love the picture of my table blessing yours and your table blessing mine. In context of our daughters, imagine a young woman coming home from school and finding her mom sitting at the kitchen table with friends. Imagine there being enough comfort and confidence in the room for this young girl to nestle into the table and conversation, because unfortunately this is not the experience of many. I remember driving my daughter, Laura, home from school one day and she said, "Mum"—that's the Aussie way—"I love you." Then she said, "It's so sad, Mum, because there are so many girls at school who hate their mums."

So there in this early pioneering tent setting was a living, breathing picture of what Sisterhood is truly about. It sits in my memory as beautiful, tender, and important, and I am so glad the Spirit of God allowed me to remember this moment as I write of the wonder years of Colour. It's important because future generations are important—without them this particular story ends with me and a handful of my friends.

Waterfalls, Daughters, and the Future

I called this chapter "Waterfalls and Flags" for a reason, because the photo shoot that captured the girls on the beach with the billowing flag also captured another important image. The photography team had taken my own Laura and a handful of her friends to the outskirts of Sydney, where they had found an amazing waterfall. The girls were young, and when I consider it now they were Miss Sisterhood in every sense of the word—it's just that we hadn't invented the language of Miss Sisterhood yet. (Miss Sisterhood encompasses the Sisterhood program for school-age girls.)

Wearing colorful cowboy hats, they were standing on the edge of the waterfall, shoulder to shoulder with arms wrapped around one another. This photograph captured innocent youthfulness; it captured young friendship and connection; it captured a camaraderie and devotion that would go the distance and be felt by the generation following them—a generation who at the time of this photo were probably at their mother's breast or in kindergarten.

Psalm 45 speaks of King's daughters and poetically tells how "she is led to the king, followed by her virgin companions" (Ps. 45:14 MSG). I had placed this verse over the waterfall image because it captures these truths beautifully. The point is not actually virginity (although that is an important subject)—the point is raising a generation of young women who will mature with wisdom and age and compel others to follow confidently in their footsteps and ultimately follow them into relationship with the King of heaven.

Generations are vitally important, and so also is *appreciation of and devotion to one's nation.*

Without love for one's nation, land, and place of planting we are unable to truly reach for all that God intends, which brings me back to Rachel. She was obviously here in the perfect timing of God. Not only did she cast a stunning stroke of color and create a worthy freeze-frame moment for me in the marquee (relating to the generations), God used her in a unique way in the Hub Auditorium the next evening, in context of national love and responsibility.

Bobbie, You Can Vote on This

She had taught what was on her heart, and had then chosen to walk around and interact with the 1,500 or so women in the room. From where I sat, she was to my left on the raised landing, when all of a sudden she paused, lifted her voice, and with unusual authority, clarity, and precision prophesied into the atmosphere. She said: *"You can vote on this . . .* The Spirit of the Lord says you can vote on this!" And then, without blinking an eye, she resumed whatever she was doing among the girls. It felt completely random and strangely disconnected from all that was happening.

In my mind the word didn't seem to be for anyone specific up there on my left—it felt like she was simply declaring it into the atmosphere. I'm not sure that anyone else understood the strange statement, but I felt that I did. As I let the words resonate for a second, it was like my mind elevated into the heavens where God might sit looking down at the orbit and sphere of Earth. It felt like God was saying:

YOU CAN VOTE ON THIS.

You can vote. You can decide, Bobbie, if you want to run with this or not.

You don't have to say yes, but I'm looking from heaven to Earth right now.

I'm looking for a company of believers,
a company of women, a nation who are going to say YES!

Yes to my will,

Yes to my heart,

Yes to my strategy,

Yes to my desire for my beloved daughters,

Yes to being a host, a church, a nation who are going to understand my heart for my daughters and my heart for humanity.

YOU CAN VOTE. I won't make you; it's your decision!

Please don't consider me crazy, but in that moment when mind and heart are caught in something that feels tangibly divine, I said yes! I volunteered. I volunteered myself, I volunteered my church, I volunteered the women of Hillsong, I volunteered my nation—I volunteered Australia!

Hilarious when I actually think about it. I don't think I literally put my hand up, but in my heart I did! It wasn't a desperate case of "pick me, pick me"—it was a case of simply saying yes. Yes to a King who seemed to be speaking to the very depths of my soul.

The Bible says several times that God's eyes scout the earth looking for those who understand: "The LORD looks down from heaven on the children of man, to see if there are any who understand, who seek after God" (Ps. 14:2 ESV). I'm confident this verse has applied to many things over many centuries, but on this occasion it felt like God was in highest heaven, far above the nations, looking for a company of believers who were going to take the value, rescue, and redemption of His daughters seriously.

From High Above

Imagine with me His eyes roaming the earth that night. Have you ever seen images of planet Earth from outer space when darkness falls? The glow of city lights and populated areas looks amazing— imagine God pondering this question from highest heaven: *Who is going to understand! Who is going to roll up their sleeves, count the cost, pay the price? Who is going to influence and rescue the daughters that I know are struggling right now? Who is going to pay attention to those weeping behind closed doors or in closed nations? Who is going to step into the aftermath of past and present killing fields? Who is going to change the generational curses that oppress and bind My girls? Who is going to rescue the precious ones who right now are looking into this night sky and are wondering if I exist, if I care? Who is going to intervene for the one being raped or held captive, for the one being stalked for purposes she was never created to endure? Who is going to pray? Who is going to care?*

I can imagine God scouting the earth that night. His eyes saw the vast continent of Australia spread before Him—the lights of Sydney drew his attention. Then a suburb stands out, where several thousand of his daughters are gathered. He knows exactly from where they all come; He knows the intricate details of their lives and the plans He has for each of them. He knows that some are leaders, others are influencers, and all carry untapped potential. He sees something within them that is willing. Perhaps that willingness is unrefined and undeveloped, but if He posed the question, would the response be a resounding YES?

Some may smile at my vivid imagination, but that's actually how it felt. That night I said yes, and that night I decided.

I decided at a personal level to commit my own heart and the women of our house—Hillsong. As their pastor and leader, I am responsible and called to lead them as women of God. I committed us to a cause greater than ourselves. By God's grace, the women of Hillsong will together go down in history as having cared for the welfare and plight of feminine humankind.

And I decided for our nation. At the time, I had been empowered to bring vision and leadership to the women of our denominational fellowship. I couldn't legislate that every church and every woman within those churches would align, but I would do my best to present the vision and example it, in and through my own girls and the conference.

And somewhere in this crazy mix of innocence, humility of heart, faith, and trepidation, I believe God used the vote to inspire other women from other places to do likewise. Many have gone forward, volunteering their own heart and their sphere of influence.

Heaven's Chronicles

History's pages and heaven's chronicles record life. I don't completely know what heaven has scribed thus far about this Sisterhood story, but my desire remains that the women of Australia (the land of my planting and my entrusted responsibility) will be recorded as having made a difference of some kind. My desire is that we would use well our "for such a time as this" (Esther 4:14) and not present in heaven one day, guilty of not having tried or given our best. Of course, the reach of Hillsong is broader these days than Australia alone, but these were my convictions around the turn of the new millennium.

God strategically watches over everything we do. Somewhere in this mix of time, space, and experience, He was stirring our hearts and preparing our willingness to say yes to what lay ahead. I recall a newspaper article. It was a weekend paper and it talked about the "27 million slaves that exist today." The horror of human slavery is a centuries-old issue, but around that time it definitely wasn't front-page news and didn't have the exposure it has today. I remember staring at the article for some length of time. And then at my kitchen table, I looked up and said, "Lord, we have to do something about this." At the time, I had no clue where or how to begin and, probably like many, felt helpless and incapable—but God saw the concern and willingness and heard the prayer. Years later, this same Sisterhood I have been laboring to write about would begin to play a very strategic role in bringing both awareness and solution to this mammoth need.

"Buy-in" and Willingness

God knew what he was asking when Rachel, as a faithful servant of the Lord, said, "You can vote on this." He knew the potential He had placed within us to bring correction and solution to the many issues presenting, but as with all things, he needed "buy-in." He needed a company of willing hearts prepared to volunteer their heart, gifting, talent, time, and resources—and most importantly, he needed a willingness to be broken for the plight of others.

The wonder years were achieving their purpose and the stakes were about to rise—and a growing bunch of us were in. The daughters were awake and there was movement in the camp. The troops were finding the reason for their existence, and the women Jesus had been waiting for were literally assembling. The real fun and games were about to begin.

What lay ahead wasn't for the fainthearted, timid, or fearful. At times it would be emotionally exhausting and yet exhilarating. Battle lines had been drawn by a loving God in heaven, and His darling daughters were about to step up and commit like never before. We were about to put on the armor of God in new and powerful ways and learn from those in the field, who would teach us much about courage and tenacity. The fight between good and evil, justice and injustice, light and darkness was about to begin anew and afresh on our watch.

Many of us were still inexperienced, but the days ahead were about to take us beyond our wildest imaginings and propel us into new chapters of God's will for our lives. Another world was beckoning and our eyes were open. The ancient words to Queen Esther were also resonating: "For if you keep silent at this time, relief and deliverance will rise for the Jews from another place, but you and your father's house will perish. And who knows whether you have not come to the kingdom *for such a time as this?*" (Esther 4:14 ESV, emphasis mine).

My prayer for you, dear reader, is that like Queen Esther you are sensing afresh His call upon your life, and that these words we are sharing within these pages are fanning that flame within you. Chapter 14 is one of my favorites. Go grab a coffee or tea and come with me as we begin to enter a new era within the story.

fourteen

THE REAL WORLD BECKONS

(The Dots)

When I met Brian we were both babies.

I was sixteen going on seventeen and he was nineteen going on twenty. For anyone thinking, "Do I hear the sound of music and was Julie Andrews in the mix?" the answer is no. We were not on the Swiss-German border. We were on the other side of the planet in little old New Zealand—land of sheep and sports lovers, Hobbits, and *The Lord of the Rings* movie adventures.

We met on a beach. I was in a white bikini, tanned as the ace of spades, with long black hair that went past my butt. "Lanky-legs Houston" came up and over the sand dune with his mate Murray, and ever so spiritually said, "I bags her." Now in some cultures that possibly sounds awful, but back then it simply meant "I saw her first, I choose her." I (randomly) bought him an ice cream, we fell in love, and church bells rang about four years later. Nothing about our young lives was particularly grand or exotic.

We cleaned the canteen and men's toilets at Ford Motors to save money for our wedding, rented a fairly ordinary first house, and we borrowed Brian's mom's little blue car for a honeymoon around the South Island of New Zealand. On that honeymoon we stayed in motels and camping cabins. We bunked down on his parents' living-room floor two nights into our marriage (imagine that), and spent a couple of nights staying with Brian's mates around the South Island—his friends would move out and let us have their single bed.

I'm not wounded by the experience (LOL), except for the interisland ferry crossing that resembled a sequel to the movie *Titanic*—but that's another story. We were in love and it didn't matter that our honeymoon was nothing like the exotic honeymoons I often hear young people taking today.

It also didn't matter that when we started out in ministry we never took holidays or vacation time for about seven years or so.

To be honest, I don't think I even noticed that we weren't taking vacations till we moved out to the Hills District of Sydney to pioneer what is now Hillsong Church and employed our first-ever associate pastor, who was (in a lovely way) quite pedantic about entering his four weeks of vacation leave onto the planning calendar. It may have been at that point that I ventured into Brian's office and ever so gently said, "Darling, do you think we should have holidays also?"

As already shared, the early days of our marriage were spent in gorgeous and exciting Sydney. We were pioneering the church with his parents, and we were happily living by faith. Brian cleaned shop-front windows for two dollars a window in Sydney's prestigious Paddington, and we had live-in boarders to help pay the rent and put food on the table. Every holiday season was the same—my man kissed the babies and me good-bye and drove off to preach at Christmas or Easter camps for young people and others.

All this is to say that God watches the sacrifices made and has a remarkable ability to cause you to reap in places you would never have imagined. In our early years, our vacations may have been rare and humble, but in recent times God has blessed us with vacation locations and moments of blessing that I am convinced are part of his reward, "exceeding abundantly above" those early years of sacrifice (Eph. 3:20 JUB).

On that note, it's remarkable how an e-mail and a rescheduled flight on one of those magnificent trips are all it takes for heaven to join two massive dots in a master plan. That is exactly what happened—one was on the romantic coastline of Italy, and one was in a remote corner of Canada. Both related to a continent and a people who were in yet another corner of the earth.

Location, Location

I never imagined that loving and leading our little Aussie church would take us to exotic and grand places. I never imagined we'd have spiritual sons and daughters or rooms in the Hillsong house that were in London, Paris, and New York, to name but a few. I never imagined that working and ministering in the Northern Hemisphere (hosting our European conferences) would allow us to take rest and relaxation in beautiful and romantic settings like the coastline of Italy.

And so it was one year that on that Italian coastline I found myself responding to an e-mail. We had just had a beautiful midyear break in a part of the world that God obviously had fun creating—we had soaked up the sunshine, swum in the gorgeous waters, and probably eaten too much pasta. We were feeling refreshed, and it was our last day of vacation. I opened my BlackBerry and saw an e-mail from one of the great girls at home in context of Hillsongwomen, which, as already mentioned, was our weekly chick meeting. She said words to this effect: "Bobbie, the girls have done a great job leading... but we are ready for you to come home and lead the charge."

I remember standing on the cool Italian tiles of our room—the sun was shining and a light summer breeze caught the sheer floor-to-ceiling curtains of the little French-style door that opened to the balcony. In the perfection of this setting, I replied: "Donna, it's been amazing but I'm ready to come home. The real world beckons." As I hit the send button, I felt God's Spirit speak so clearly and softly in my ear: "YES, because there are children to rescue and hurting people to minister to."

I will pause here to say that hearing God speak and bring direction in one's life is often as simple as this. It's the "still small voice" (1 Kings 19:12 KJV) that seemingly comes from nowhere and yet resonates within. Of course, not every random thought that passes through our often fertile minds is God's voice. But with time you can learn to discern, and with time it will outwork itself with good fruit that bears witness that what you heard was indeed the leading of God's Spirit.

Back to the e-mail moment: As lovely as this Italian setting was, as beautiful as the planet can be, as much as it is actually okay to be blessed and experience blessing, the real world still exists and the real world still beckons.

My husband frequently reminds our congregation that "we are blessed to be a blessing." This conviction is at the core of our belief and mission as a church. Our own lives are given and spent on the betterment of others, and God, knowing this, had blessed us that year with some much-needed rest and relaxation. He had allowed us to breathe and replenish our souls in the most beautiful of settings—and yet He also knew where our true hearts lay.

As I acknowledged to my friend Donna that we were indeed ready to come home and put our hand again to the plough of the real world, the Holy Spirit stepped in with yet another aspect to this Sisterhood story: "Orphans to rescue, sisters to come alongside, nations to believe in." I knew exactly what He was saying, and I returned home holding these words that related to children, sisters, and nations in my spirit.

Hazel's Rainbow

It was in the context of this new season unfolding that two more events would join the dots that heaven had masterminded.

Brian had received and accepted a ministry invitation to Canada. There was an established denomination keen for Brian to come and speak into their lives. By their own admission, they were struggling with vision and direction and wanted what was upon Brian's life and leadership to help them. We went, gave our best, and shared what we had to offer. The conference was in the easternmost corner of Canada, and once it was over we were keen to get home.

We rose at four a.m. to catch the flight from St. John's, Newfoundland, to Los Angeles, and then onward to Sydney the next evening. When we arrived at the airport, we heard what no traveler enjoys hearing—the flight had been delayed. Till midday! Sigh, breathe, and slump your shoulders. The airport wasn't exactly a thriving metropolis of shops or restaurants, so what would we do to pass that many hours? Then a stroke of genius hit us—our room was still available at the hotel. Let's head back and go back to bed! We headed curbside to catch a taxi. As we hailed the first available cab, another couple were also planning to do exactly the same. We looked at each other and decided to share the ride.

Squashed in together, we introduced ourselves as the dawn light began to filter through the clouds. Their names were Gary and Marilyn Skinner. They were missionaries to Uganda with the denomination we were visiting and apparently hadn't been home to their annual conference for many years. However, something had compelled them to return for this one. They were complimentary of our ministry at the conference, and during the cab ride together we told them that we were headed back to Australia for one week, and then we were going to Kampala, Uganda, to visit for the first time with our Compassion (child sponsorship) children there.

Coincidence—or providence?

The Skinners graciously extended an invitation: "When you arrive in Kampala, call us and we'll have dinner together." Invitation accepted, we all unloaded out of the cab and headed for our still-unmade beds in the hotel. Midday came and we were on that plane to Los Angeles.

The delay turned into about nineteen hours, which made us late to participate in Phil and Holly Wagner's twentieth-anniversary church celebrations. As the plane landed and began to taxi toward the gate in LA, Brian opened his phone. I was wedged between travelers eager to exit, and I will never forget his words from behind me: "My mother has just had a heart attack. She's in a coma." The next twenty-four hours and the next seven days were a whirlwind.

We couldn't change our flights to fly home urgently, so Brian spoke for the Wagners' normal Sunday services the next morning and then we caught the evening flight home. We arrived Tuesday morning and raced north to where Brian's dear mother lay in a coma. She was eighty-three years of age. She had collapsed at McDonald's that Sunday morning on her way to church, and the family were desperate for Brian to arrive and help them over the emotional line of what to do next. The next day (Wednesday), as a giant rainbow came to rest over the hospital, Hazel Winifred Houston slipped into eternity with her daughters gathered beside her.

We buried her and celebrated her stoic life two days later, and then on Saturday we left for Uganda. In retrospect, we had every reason to cancel. My husband had lost his mother, the family was grieving, and our own daughter, Laura, was having her own little teenage meltdown. But for some bizarre reason we chose to go ahead with the African trip, albeit now with Laura in tow. Brian had called those organizing the trip and had said that unless there was room for Laura, we could not come. What she was facing as a young woman needed our attention as much as the children we were planning to visit and help in Africa.

The geographic and destiny dots were being joined by an unseen force. In Italy, God had dropped new language into my spirit regarding the future of the Sisterhood. In Canada, he brought two Australians and two African missionaries halfway across the earth and orchestrated a "chance meeting" in what felt like a remote corner of the planet. He had allowed (or taken advantage of) a delayed flight to facilitate a collision of lives on a curbside. He had overshadowed a conversation in a taxi and prompted a dinner invitation that would become a divine appointment.

In Australia, the enemy had sought to interfere and sabotage the connections in play by creating angst and unrest in our daughter (another story for another time), and circumstances had intensified because of the death and passing of our beloved mother.

Despite all that, we pressed through and engaged a divine connection and relationship that would prove so critical to the vision of Sisterhood and what God knew we were capable of. He was joining some pivotal dots in the story—and any who have been on this Colour journey with me will know what I am writing of.

Hearts Knit

My life, heart, and soul knit that weekend in Uganda to a world far removed from our normal borders.

We arrived in Kampala tired and weary after an exhausting seven days, but we still kept our dinner engagement that evening. Sitting in a local restaurant with the Skinners, I listened intently to the life of the petite Canadian missionary. She was joyful, positive, and full of vision. As we sat eating (and trying to keep our eyelids open), she was also full of stories—stories of life as young, naive missionaries in Uganda; stories of life with a young family in the terror of the Milton Obote regime, a man who killed more people than Idi Amin; stories of faith and tenacity in the face of extreme challenge; and stories of ambush and guns held to her head as she leant on the sovereignty of her God. What was remarkable was her ability to tell such stories with joy—at one point I remember thinking, "Did she just say they held a gun to her head and threatened her life... and did she just burst into joyful laughter telling about it?"

Obviously God had just introduced me to a whole new world, and something within me thought this girl would be amazing at Colour. She was a strong, gutsy woman of faith who had experienced and endured much. She was definitely a missionary, but she didn't fit the mold of what some might (wrongly) perceive as "a missionary." I sat enthralled and intrigued, but I had no idea of what was really within this woman, nor did I fully comprehend that the words I had received a few weeks earlier in Italy, about children to rescue and hurting people to minister to, would be so intrinsically connected to this newfound friend. The fun and adventures had begun.

The Equation

God had us in the right place, at the right time, with the right people, and destiny was again in motion. God's Spirit had literally taken us around the world and back again in order that new friendship, partnership, and more importantly strategy could fall into place.

The Skinners had apparently been praying for divine alliance. They had faithfully served God in Uganda for near twenty years. They had carved out a phenomenal church and ministry, and God had brought thousands of orphaned children into their care. Yet, by their own admission, they had hit a ceiling and needed help if the expansiveness of their vision was to become reality. As they had learned to do on many an occasion, they went to their knees, looked heavenward, and asked God for help. God looked down, saw the potential in certain players (them and us), and connected the dots.

As far as Brian and I were concerned, God knew our lives and ministry. He knew our strength and integrity as a church, and He knew our sphere of reach and influence with our conferences. He knew that our lives would be a perfect fit with the Skinners and that our entrusted platform of influence would bless their entrusted platform of influence, so yet again the pieces were being woven together.

He took the dynamics of two ministries and joined them in a divine union that would provide new strategy in the rescue, redemption, and care of children and others who were important to Him. As our friendship grew, an equation took shape within my spirit that helped me understand what God was doing: Years + Strength + Influence = Strategy!

I believe God wanted to showcase to the Body of Christ and to secular governing bodies what can happen when unity and cohesion exist. Sadly, some people can become negatively territorial in their endeavors to change the world—wanting to run their own show, start their own foundations, NGOs, or whatever. Please hear me correctly when I say that there is nothing inherently wrong with this—and if you have been inspired to do it, then more power to you—but it is also true to say that sometimes God has had the right players in the right field for many years, and all He wants is for others to take their unique strength and influence and *add* it to what He is already doing.

Sometimes endless and competing parallel responses do nothing but weaken the overall plan. If all of us—especially those who believe that the church in coming days is going to be a fabulous force for good—are going to effectively meet the mammoth needs of the impoverished, marginalized, and forgotten, we need to discern wisely. We need to know when to initiate new responses and we need to know when to find contentment in working alongside those already in the field, regardless of whether the workers or organizations are faith-based or not. A delicate subject but nevertheless worth pondering, because I believe God's higher plan is for all of us (faith-based or other) to work together in unity for the well-being of humanity.

Another Invitation

I end this chapter and this part of the story with another e-mail—an e-mail of invitation.

I went home to Sydney and decided to invite the cute Canadian missionary to be a speaker at our next Colour. Again, I thought she would simply give inspiration and courage to the many leaders and pastors' wives attending. Children were already an important part of our collective vision as a church and conference, and we had a strong relationship with Compassion, but there were countless other children that God had on His mind also.

Marilyn's office received the e-mail, but before she opened it, her husband, Gary, got to it first. He read the invitation and replied, "Yes." He knew that if his little wife saw it first, she would decline. She may have been an exceptional missionary, she may have been able to lead a brilliant ministry to the impoverished and orphaned, she may have been able to lead a church that measured at the time eighteen thousand, but in her own words, she had "never preached before." Had she seen the invitation, she would have declined in fear. So Gary replied yes on her behalf.

And so it was that, with much love and affection, we welcomed the lovely Marilyn into our world and hearts. As she graced my

2004 platform and spoke her first-ever sermon, what came with her was a whole new world of discovery. "Orphans to rescue, sisters to come alongside, and nations to believe in" began to be etched not only into our language but also our hearts.

What would unfold over the next few years was a grand company of women who would unite in friendship and undertake and facilitate the support of hundreds of women and children in Africa. As God joined the dots and as He continued to gather everyday women from far and wide, He knew that if we heard the cry of the afflicted we would respond and become a formidable force in their rescue. Certain lines in the sand were about to be drawn and crossed, in both the natural and spiritual realm.

On a personal note, dear friend, I hope that your own heart is being reminded of God at work in your own story and circumstance. Often we don't immediately perceive or understand the master strokes taking shape, but with time, distance, and good old patience, it is remarkable how obvious His hand is in all our lives. I pray that you are inspired to step back a little and appreciate anew the divine (people) connections at work in your life. I hope this book and this story are one of them, or at least a stroke of color on the canvas.

PART THREE

· · ·

The Sisterhood

fifteen

DID SOMEONE JUST FAINT?

(The Lines)

I doubt that any war against injustice has ever been declared, fought, or won without first a line being drawn in the sand that says, "Enough now…this reign of terror, injustice, and ill-doing must end!"

Jesus drew a line in the sand—in fact, He drew many.

One such moment is recorded in the Gospel of John and tells of a woman in the hands of her accusers. Regardless of innocence or guilt, she is thrown at Jesus' feet with a judgment of "guilty." In plain sight of everyone, the cruel religious authorities of the day say, "Teacher, this woman was caught red-handed in the act of adultery. Moses, in the Law, gives orders to stone such persons. What do you say?" (John 8:4–5 MSG).

The tone in which Jesus replied is not recorded, but His words are: "He that is without sin among you, let him first cast a stone at her" (John 8:7 KJV). He then knelt and wrote in the stony sand—what he wrote remains a mystery that many an inquiring mind and theologian has speculated upon for centuries. Perhaps we will never know.

Perhaps what He wrote was personal and pertained only to her accusers, because the story tells how they slowly withdrew. Perhaps

He quietly yet poignantly revealed their flaws, failings, and vulnerability. Perhaps He wrote of the Father's great love, or something that silenced the real enemy and real accuser of Earth's beloved sons and daughters. Whatever happened in the shadow of that Temple Mount, a line between right and wrong, condemnation and forgiveness was drawn. Kindness and grace prevailed, and the death of a broken woman condemned to a savage stoning was averted.

When the same Jesus selflessly died for you and me, He also drew a line in the sand—a line that marked our rescue and redemption. It was a line stained red with holy and precious blood, a line that began at the cross of Calvary and now stretches far into eternity. For multiplied millions the world over, it has become the scarlet thread of redemption, an undeniable lifeline that wraps itself around the human soul and anchors itself (and them) within the incorruptible veil of His eternal presence.

It's also a battle line, a battle line that will forever remind the enemy that he has lost and Christ has won. I believe that we have been commissioned and empowered to do the same—to draw battle lines in both the natural and spiritual realm that will mark injustice upon the earth as "not acceptable, not okay, and no longer permissible."

And so it was, on a certain normal and seemingly unspectacular Thursday in our local Aussie Sisterhood, that God's Spirit drew a line in the sand for us—a line of greater understanding and revelation, a line of compassion and commissioning that would create *a shift in our hearts.*

It was 2004, and from the comfort of Sydney's leafy and peaceful northern suburbs, we were carried into the everyday village life of a young family in a faraway continent—Africa. I had been reading an array of books that had flooded the market about life in other cultures. Many had to do with centuries-old lifestyles and customs that to the Western world could be mysterious, strange, and even disturbing. This particular book, *Slave: My True Story* by Mende Nazer, lovingly captured the carefree existence of a young girl in Africa—a little girl who loved simple village life and who frolicked and played with her siblings and friends, a little girl who felt the love of her parents, a little girl with dreams and aspirations, a little girl who was wide-eyed with childlike wonder at her world.

Her home in a typical rural-African mud-hut setting may have seemed humble by some standards, but what I loved and was being enlightened to was the normality of a family life that, in all truthfulness, was no different from ours. Family love was strong, life lessons were in play, and her parents desired only the best for their children. And then I turned a page in the story—and a new chapter began.

It was to prove a new chapter not only for this young African girl but also for me—a new chapter not only for this sweet, innocent child who was maturing into womanhood but also for our entire Sisterhood, who were—whether we realized it or not—about to mature in understanding and empathy.

The Cutting

This young girl had come of age and was about to be "cut." As was the tradition of her culture, it was her time—her time to be marked or sealed for womanhood, her time to experience what every woman down through her family had experienced, her time to be prepared for purity, marriage, and destiny. As I read this little girl's story, my heart enlarged and then broke.

I was well aware that female circumcision existed. I was well aware that cultural traditions surround this practice, in which young female human flesh is cut away, ensuring and proving virginity on the marriage day. It is a tradition that has prevailed in many cultures for many centuries—but what I was not prepared for was the human story and the human emotion surrounding this one act and this one particular family.

And so, on this particular Thursday morning, I had chosen to include this chapter of her life in my teaching. I wanted our girls to understand and empathize. I wanted them to experience what I had just experienced reading her story. How could any of us, who have never been in such a situation, begin to understand the complexity, confusion, and agony of such an experience? Had I not read this little girl's graphic firsthand story, female genital mutilation would have remained for me a disturbing statistic of an oftentimes bewildering world—a statistic that we might read about and cringe over, wondering perhaps, "How could this still happen in a modern and sophisticated world?"

And personally, I couldn't possibly understand. I was raised in a completely different environment. The traditions of my land and upbringing would have abhorred this practice. My parents loved me, and my father would have literally died protecting me from such a traumatic experience. But then, this little girl's parents also loved her, and her father in his own way also saw his child as a princess worthy of protection—yet tradition and culture demanded her cutting.

Empathy, Not Judgment

And so it was in this context of empathy (and not judgment) that I asked my Sisterhood girls to sit back and allow me to read something to them. I opened the book and silently asked the Holy Spirit to help me: "Lord, please help me read this with grace and conviction... Please help me to do justice to this child's story... Please help us to understand in a manner worthy of your heart towards this reality."

My teaching series in and around this time was called "Injustice

Moves Her." My humble desire was that God would begin to move our hearts from places of comfort to discomfort; that we would be moved with compassion for the plight and lives of others; and that compassion would then, in turn, lead us to be agents of change. With determined focus, I opened the autobiography to the chapter marked and began to read.

As the reality of her formidable day of cutting took shape before my girls, I could feel the atmosphere in the room thicken and intensify. If a pin had dropped, I'm sure we would have heard it. God's Spirit was definitely present. I continued.

As her father ceremoniously took solace in the men's hut of the village, her mother and older sisters took this young girl to where her cutting would take place. She was around the age of twelve. "The woman" (the village midwife) arrived from working in the fields. Unlike most surgical procedures in Western culture, there was no clinic involved. No pristine waiting room, no pictures on the wall to soothe a young child's heart. No promise of a lollipop or other reward if you will "be a good girl" while an anesthetic is gently administered. No sterilization of scalpel or instruments. As is the case for thousands of young girls subjected to this tradition, the cutting happens in your parents' hut, on a rock, or in the wilderness.

As I read aloud, Mende (the young girl) described how her heart and mind trembled with confusion and fear. She told of the onset of terror as "the woman" crouched between her legs and then held them open. She described the absolute lack of kindness as the grubby woman unwrapped a primitive blade, then grabbed her tender flesh and sliced.

The girl cried out in horror as excruciating pain surged through her body. As blood gushed down her thighs and legs, her mother and sisters held her down. For an hour, the woman cut and sliced away at her delicate young flesh—and then, without a word of comfort or encouragement, she threaded a rusty needle and sewed together what was left of a twelve-year-old vagina, leaving only a small opening.

Amid the burning agony and blinding reality of what was happening to her, her flesh and womanhood was thrown into the dirt and then callously buried and stomped upon. As I pressed on to read aloud what ensued thereafter in the hut, my peripheral vision could see something was happening in the room among my own girls. I sensed something was amiss but I couldn't stop. I was committed to the reading, regardless of how graphic or disturbing it was, but in my subconscious a question flashed: "Did someone just faint? Did Rachel on the front row just keel over into the lap of the woman next to her?"

I know this could almost sound comical (and in retrospect it almost is), but in that moment of sharing the story and plight of another, something was happening in the atmosphere of the room and the realm of our hearts.

Indeed, what had happened (unbeknownst to me) is that not only had one woman fainted on the front row, but *seven women had fainted* in various parts of the auditorium. And not only that, phones strangely started ringing, and all manner of disturbance began unsettling the atmosphere. I pressed on for reasons I didn't really fathom at the time—all I knew was that I was in a zone and I wasn't about to abort. I stopped only when I heard a woman cry out.

I looked up and saw something unusual in our church setting: A woman had stood up, stepped out into the aisle, and was slowly and falteringly walking toward me. She was visibly distressed, which in turned disturbed those watching. It all happened in a split second, but I recall my team and ushers looking at me as if to say, *Should we stop her?* I motioned them to leave her.

"It's okay, girls. It's okay. Everyone be still. Be still, girls...I know this is difficult...but we need to hear this." As I reflect, I wasn't only stilling the unsettled hearts of my beloved Sisterhood; I felt I was stilling the spiritual atmosphere swirling around us. I then beckoned the obviously distressed woman to say what she needed to say.

The woman approaching me was a midwife, and her gentle outcry was, "This happens. I'm a midwife. I see this. It's horrible. The doctors have to undo this, mend this. We see this. This doesn't just happen in faraway places. This happens here and now in our cities."

I understood.

I hadn't just read a disturbing story about a disturbing reality that happens to others. God's Spirit was stirring us and He was making us vehemently aware of something that His daughters and our sisters had undergone for centuries and are still undergoing today. He was helping us to understand and empathize (empathy means identifying with and leaning into the suffering of another). A line was being drawn in the sand—a line that would define us in that moment and define us for the days ahead.

Awareness Hurts

The blade hurts, but so also does true awareness. That reading had suddenly made us aware—more aware than was comfortable for many. We had been transported into the world of another and had not merely read or heard about it, we had felt it—we had *felt* the confusion, we had *felt* the blade, we had *felt* the pain!

We respectfully and nervously joked afterward about the girls fainting. To be honest, people, fainting isn't the issue. I have a friend whose husband, Nicolas, practically faints if you mention the word "aspirin"—God love him. At the prenatal classes of their first child, the midwife teacher held up a pink crocheted uterus to explain the birth process and a sudden wave of nausea almost took Nicolas out.

I fainted once. We had been out boating and Brian was trying to manually maneuver our little ski boat into a tight corner of our driveway. The drive was slippery and he suddenly started sliding uncontrollably forward with the boat. I was unloading the picnic paraphernalia from the car and could see that the boat was about to crash into the garage wall. I obviously had been listening to my own preaching about "Proverbs 31 strength," because a delusional spirit of Superwoman came over me—in a flash of complete and utter stupidity, I wedged myself between the garage and the sliding boat, thinking I could stop it with my puny arms. Consequently, the boat smashed my arm into the wall and I felt tendons or bones ping and break. I recall prancing around the garage in agony, thinking "I don't have time for a broken arm, I don't have time for a broken arm"—and then I fainted.

I awakened to my son Ben standing over me saying, "Mum. Mum. Dad's not angry with you, he's just upset you are hurt." As I lay there thinking "Did I just faint?" I could hear Brian. He was still holding the boat on the slippery drive and was yelling "Why did you do that? Why did you do that? . . . That was the most *stupid* thing ever."

Yes. So life and fainting (and strange responses from beloved husbands) can happen to the best of us. On that Thursday morning in Sydney, while a few of us may have fainted literally, all of us fainted in heart and spirit. Our hearts were torn and exposed, and yet from that place of tearing, from that place of deep and raw empathy, many of us stood up with a different determination to be our sisters' keepers and address some of the issues that face our world.

Compassion Is Costly

Change never occurs without first a willingness to be made aware— and willingness to be made aware is the catalyst of all change.

I recount this story not to make judgment upon the cultures or traditions of others, although I believe that female circumcision and all it entails thereafter for the girls and women involved is not how a loving Creator intended it. I recount this moment because in our Sisterhood journey, God was looking for and needing a host of girls who would allow their hearts to move beyond statistics to the real lives and real hearts within the statistics.

I believe there are pivotal moments in all our lives that are like the lines I've been writing about—moments where awareness is heightened and compassion is ignited, moments where revelation about a certain subject or issue suddenly leaves us with no option but to change or respond differently. In that sense, godly compassion is costly.

I tagged this chapter "The Lines" because God's desire for all humanity is pleasant lines, not brutal or harsh ones. In Psalm 16 the ancient psalmist writes, "The lines have fallen for me in pleasant places; yes, I have a good heritage" (Ps. 16:6 AMP).

This Psalm has always held an affectionate place in my heart. As a young girl, I camped on these verses and simply believed the promise within them. I somehow felt that the lines surrounding my life were blessed and would always be blessed because I had made a conscious decision to live according to the goodness of God, which ultimately becomes the framework of blessed heritage.

Sometimes the devil-enemy draws battle lines around our lives in a bid to do the opposite. The Bible is clear that he exists to steal, kill, destroy, maim, and create dysfunction (see John 10:10). We in turn need to draw battle lines around his battle lines—battle lines that also rally the troops to fight for and on behalf of others. Proverbs 31 commands us to raise our voice for those without voice and to stand in the gap of those who have no rights.

I believe that notable day at Sisterhood saw a band of women rise up and cross a line. In fact, one of my dear friends said, "Bobbie, today you drew a line in the sand. You crossed it...and we came with you." Our hearts were open to movement. We were open to the prompting of His Spirit and we had crossed a line (one of what would become many) that said, "We are no longer content to be content." If there was a cry to be heard, our feminine, maternal, awakening hearts were being fine-tuned to hear it.

Mende's Cry

Without doubt, we witnessed a few twists and turns that day, and I ended my storytelling and teaching around the rest of this little girl's story. Mende was later taken captive by a marauding band of Arab rebels, and she tragically became one of today's slave statistics. She was smuggled to England.

As I recounted her story and considered the many others like hers, I tried to imagine the cry of her heart in the depths of her night season. I imagined her and others trapped in darkness and containment. I imagined them perhaps looking at the night sky and wondering, "Is there a God in heaven who hears, who cares—is there a God capable of rescue?"

Pondering their plight, I imagined the canopy of their literal night sky. I realized that the stars and moon they in their sadness and captivity observe are, for the most part, the same stars and moon we observe in our freedom and liberty—the same stars, the same moon, the same God above all.

Regardless of redemption or not (or religion or not), this same God hears any cry offered from the human heart. From highest heaven, He hears. In ancient times He heard the desperate outcry of the children of Israel, who had been held in harsh captivity for four hundred years—the Bible actually says that their cry ascended to Him (see Exod. 2:23). He heard, He had a strategy, and He had a plan. All He needed was someone willing to step into that strategy, align their heart, and simply be available. In that ancient setting, He found and chose Moses. Moses wasn't eloquent or necessarily remarkable, but He was (eventually) willing.

I wonder if God from highest heaven isn't waiting patiently for our response and willingness. Each night, desperate souls cry out for help and rescue—are we willing to hear also and be available should God choose to involve us?

Lines in the sand are important. They separate those willing from those unwilling; they separate the players from the bystanders, the men from the boys, and the women of God from the girls.

My prayer is that you will take the Father's hand and step over whatever lines He is maturing you toward. He will never force us, but He will gently, strategically, and relentlessly urge us, because He knows what reward lies on the other side of response and obedience. Like the woman taken in adultery and thrown at Jesus' feet, take His extended hand and allow Him to lift you up. Allow Him to lift you, so that others may be lifted in turn by *your* extended hand.

As a collective Sisterhood, we had just experienced a critical next step in our awakening. Empathy was again maturing as hearts enlarged and hands fell open in a stance of surrender and availability. As many of my girls headed home to attend to housework or prepare for that happy hour when kids storm home from school, I retired to my office. I made a mental note that if I ever put this teaching into a CD series, perhaps it would be wise to add a footnote: WARNING: DO NOT LISTEN TO THIS WHILE DRIVING. I had a ghastly vision of women passing out behind the wheel as they happily listened to what was normally an uplifting message. I also wondered where God was leading.

From the comfort of my little office I had a small inkling, but from the circuit of the heavens, our glorious, kind, and compassionate God knew exactly where He was taking us—jungles, rats, rebels, and yet another marquee were visible from where He sat.

An Envelope

As I sat in the aftermath and strange afterglow of that morning, my assistant quietly brought an envelope into my office and placed it on my desk. A woman in the meeting (who, if I recall correctly, had chosen to remain anonymous) had asked that it be passed on to me. When I opened it, I quietly gasped.

On the card, she had written words to the effect that she was deeply moved, that the issues being spoken of were important, and that she herself was "a mere peasant." Her choice of words about being a peasant was a little odd, but somehow I understood and sensed that what lay ahead would touch a world where this language was not uncommon. Enclosed within the card was a check for $20,000.

At this point the (Colour) Sisterhood Foundation had zero financial resources. I had simply created and secured the foundation in obedience and had been content to sit on the idea and stir the human heart in the meantime. But that morning, it was as if heaven decided for us: "You've crossed the line—here is seed to now take this off the drawing board of your heart and into the arena of action."

sixteen

RATS, REBELS, STILETTOS, AND CLEAVAGE SEED

(The Afflicted)

A natural seed needs soil, and it's no different with spiritual seeds of destiny and calling.

Destiny seeds that will become the food and hope of many need to fall into the good soil of our hearts. However, in the parable of the sower in Matthew 13, Jesus teaches that not every seed sown by the Father brings forth—some will be snatched away before they have a chance to make a difference; some will flourish for a moment and then be lost because the depth to sustain is lacking; and some will be choked by the cares of a world that endlessly competes against the will of God on the earth. But then Jesus goes on to say that other seed will fall on other soil, which with time and nurture will go on to bring forth either a thirty-, sixty-, or hundredfold return.

I don't know about you, but I want to be a "hundredfold girl."

I want to steward as well as I can what God has entrusted, and to that end it felt like the Gardener Himself was turning the soil of our hearts in preparation for something grand He had in mind. Lessons and principles were in play, and I pray that anything we learned throughout these years will be added blessing to your story and journey.

Certain statements carry a flood of memory and color, not least these two: "Bobbie, women are stampeding in their stilettos to the tent" and "Madam, you don't just have a small infestation, you have a *kingdom of rats* in your ceiling."

Both memories relate to the territory we were entering in Africa, but the memory of the rats reminds me of two young boys whose unfettered emotion deeply affected seventeen thousand women. Allow me to give you a little background to this part of our story.

A Partnership Hatched in Heaven

Our relationship with Marilyn Skinner had grown and blossomed. She had come and spoken her first-ever message, and despite a wee meltdown on her part, involving what to share, wear, and where to get a decent haircut before landing in Australia (adorable), the Colour girls had generously leant into the passion and wonder of this little world changer.

The Skinners had facilitated a remarkable ministry to both the orphan and the widow. Over many years, they had fine-tuned their response to the massive need in Uganda by creating holistic villages, their proven strategy being to build clusters of three-bedroom brick houses, each of which became home to eight orphan children and a mother. The mother was herself often a victim of abandonment, abuse, widowhood, rejection, HIV/AIDS, or worse. These clusters then become a beautiful village family—the children and mothers are adopted forever, with the security of both a future and hope. These beautiful children (who now number in the thousands) are cared for, raised, and educated in a way that is completely inspiring—and which in turn is producing young citizens who will ultimately challenge and change the future of Uganda, and therefore Africa. The "Watoto" story (Watoto means "children" and is also the name of their ministry) is, in my opinion, one of the finest stories of collaboration and solution on the face of the earth.

The Colour Sisterhood had stepped enthusiastically into the fray with them. As Marilyn cut her teeth on her first conference message, we cut our teeth as a Sisterhood on our first global endeavor together. After she spoke at the conference, I took the stage, cast vision again relating to our Sisterhood manifesto, and seeded our first concerted humanitarian project. I don't know if it's possible to be bold and tentative at the same time, but with both realities surging through my body I posed the question: "Girls, perhaps we can combine our strength, gather our girlfriends, and build one of these houses for Marilyn? Or maybe two or three...or maybe five...or maybe (*eyes wide open and eyebrows lifted*)...*fifty!*"

In that faltering and yet faith-filled moment, new vision was cast and our first-ever tangible strategy involving the girls from Oz and the vulnerable of Africa was conceived.

The miracle is that over the years, the girls have not only built one or two houses—they've raised millions of dollars for homes in Watoto and other initiatives. I think the $20,000 seeded in the envelope (and spoken of in the previous chapter) has easily grown into the hundredfold (and more) category. We used that initial finance to create a starter kit for the girls to begin their fundraising.

We All Weep

As God began unfolding His plan among us, you didn't need to be literally on African soil to hear the cry of the afflicted. I recall a moment in the darkness of my home and study—the only light in the room was from my computer. I may have been far from violence or harm, but my heart for some reason was with my sisters in Uganda. Since meeting Marilyn, I had made it a priority to visit that distant land annually and (like many who visit Africa) had fallen deeply in love with the place.

As my own family slept, I recalled my first visit to Watoto. Gary and Marilyn had walked Brian and me through the village paths, and the perfectly kept and cared-for homes of the children and mothers were beautiful. Manicured flowers framed each front door, and behind each house fresh laundry could be seen blowing in the gentle Kampala breeze. And children—children were everywhere to be seen. We stopped for a few moments in one of the leaders' homes. As refreshments were served, we sat quietly. When overwhelmed, I tend to become quiet. Gary asked how I felt. For a moment his words hung in the air, and then I said, "Gary, I'm sorry, I think I just need to weep." I put my face in my hands and let emotion have its way.

The entire room had gone very quiet. Gary sat on the chair opposite and simply responded, "It's okay, we all weep." The grace and miracle-working goodness of God cannot be denied in these settings. When you observe a village of healthy, robust, joyful children, from newborns and toddlers to high school age and beyond, and then consider that these children were once abandoned or discarded or tragically orphaned, it is deeply overwhelming. To hold a chubby, smiling baby and then be told, "This little one was found in a public pit-latrine toilet" will render any caring heart speechless. If anything this side of eternity is a shadow of heaven's amazing grace, this ministry is.

It was in this context that my heart and mind were with my sisters. As I sat in the darkness of my study in Sydney, I found myself imagining a precious African sister in heaven, her life cut short because of disease or neglect. And then, as strange as this may sound, it felt as if I suddenly heard her speak from eternity, asking "Who will take care of my babies?"

Death is merely a transition from this life to the next. Perhaps heaven opened my ears to hear the conversation; perhaps a young woman was being ushered into heaven and her first question was: "But Lord, who will take care of my babies? Who will watch over my children?" God wasn't joking when He dropped those words about orphans to rescue into my spirit on that Italian coastline.

God was again highlighting what He needed from us—a host of willing women who would care for sisters that they may never meet this side of eternity, a host of women who would care for their left-behind babies as though they were their very own.

A Constant Reminder

As a constant reminder of these words, I have in my office a framed image that I shot from the car window as we traversed the dusty Kampala traffic. It's a photo of a Ugandan woman—it's hard to judge her age because trauma takes its toll, but she is possibly in her early thirties. She is in a rusty old wheelchair, almost antique in style. She doesn't look well; she has a baby on her lap and she is holding her head in an attitude of despair.

As my world fleetingly passed hers, I captured her world, albeit in a photo. Above the haunting image now hanging on my wall, I wrote those same words: "Who will take care of my babies?" Alongside is another image, of forty-two baby footprints (printed on gift cards that I purchased) from a clinic in Kampala where abandoned babies were brought. One day in eternity, an angel may well introduce us to a beautiful woman who lost her battle with HIV/AIDS—and perhaps the angel will tell us that it was this woman's child we helped, her child we supported, her child we made our own through collaboration with our girlfriends. Now, won't that be a grand and glorious moment? I hope they have Kleenex tissues in heaven.

Rats, Rebels, and Child Soldiers

So you may well ask, "Bobbie, where do rats, rebels, stilettos, and an odd-sounding cleavage-seed offering come into the picture?"

The two years that frame these random statements were 2007 and 2008. We had outgrown our own facilities and "the troops" were graduating into Sydney's largest indoor venue, seating twenty thousand in its raw state. The women in our nation took up the challenge and turned up in force, with the venue sold out weeks in advance. Marilyn was again among our speakers. By this time, our collaborative efforts had graduated from building houses for the orphans and widows in Kampala to ventures into the northern regions of Uganda where a fierce civil war had been raging for more than twenty years, with an evil warlord ravaging the land and the people. Joseph Kony's strategy for war was the brutal abduction of children. The child soldiers of northern Uganda had appeared on the radar of the world, and God was sending many, including the Skinners (and the Sisterhood), into the fray to face the ongoing aftermath.

I was aware of the problem, and as a church we had committed to provide financial help for the Skinners to take their much-needed ministry into the war-affected region. I also knew the Sisterhood was still within a unique season, where God was awakening, stretching, and breaking our hearts for the plight of those less fortunate, and it was in this context that I found myself preparing for Colour. As I did, I stumbled across a 2006 documentary titled *Invisible Children*, directed by Jason Russell, Bobby Bailey, and Laren Poole, American teenagers who had captured the reality of the lost children and the horrific situation on our beloved Uganda's borders.

Home Alone

Brian and I had recently commenced a renovation to our home, so we had moved into a little holiday cabin out by a local river, where I was preparing for the coming conference. It wasn't grand by any means, literally two tin sheds joined together and converted into a little weekend retreat. It was compact, to say the least, with an outside toilet and shower—a perfect retreat and party house for our growing family and the entire youth group, who loved the semicamping, wakeboarding river atmosphere. We had moved into this humble setting two weeks prior to Colour and then (of course) Brian had gone away for ten days, so home alone I was.

All was fine except for the occasional movement in the ceiling. I assumed it was simply river wildlife, the odd possum or lizard that takes up residence when a cabin is not occupied. When the pest man visited, I was given fabulous news: "Madam, you don't just have a few rats in your ceiling... you have a kingdom of rats in your ceiling."

Well I'm no sissy—you're talking to Warrior Princess Daughter, right? Rats are definitely not my favorite, but what could I do? Brian was away, Colour was bearing down like a baby in a birth canal, and I didn't have time to be precious. Organize rat bait and let's be done with the little intruders. What I didn't realize was that these little critters would take *ten days* to die—I naively thought they'd take the bait, go in search of water, and die conveniently on the riverbank. But no, no, no! For ten long days and ten long nights this "kingdom of rats" died in my ceiling and paper-thin walls. For ten days I would hear them scuttling, stampeding, and thrashing like madmen around my little cabin. I'd be asleep and then a sudden "rat death roll" next to my pillow would startle me awake.

I came home late one night and slowly opened the cabin door, half expecting a pack of revenge-seeking rats to attack me. In the remoteness of it all, I was so thankful for my two big white fluffy killer Golden Retrievers, who I confess may have been coerced into accompanying me everywhere I went around that little cabin.

Jacob's Cry

In this intense, sleep-depriving setting, I found myself watching *Invisible Children*, the thirty-minute documentary that showed the plight of these children who, to escape the threat of night raids and abduction by the rebels, would walk miles from their homes each evening to the township of Gulu and sleep wherever they could find shelter. Amid hundreds of children sleeping practically on top of each other in any public or well-lit space, this film tells the story of two young boys.

The film crew pressed into the darkened, damp corner of a public building and asked two young teenage boys what had happened to them. One of the boys started to tell his story. His brother had been taken captive and his family had been torn apart—and then he paused, and a wave of emotion descended. He began to cry, and his cry became a wail from the very depths of his being—a wail of sorrow, pain, and loss, a gut-wrenching wail of deepest, deepest despair.

The film crew went silent. When silence needed to give way to compassion, one of the interviewers leaned over and said: "It's okay, Jacob, it's okay, it's okay."

As I write this, I find my own emotions raw again. In our media-instant world, we are often exposed to suffering. Tsunamis and earthquakes, war and devastation are a constant on our television screens, but it's not often we are exposed to the traumatic cry of the human heart—and when we are, all the dynamics change! As I sat alone in my remote little rat-infested cabin, watching this film again and again and again, I found myself weeping again and again and again for these children. At times I found myself on the floor, overwhelmed with grief for the injustice and insanity of it all.

Dilemma and Quandary

Perhaps it was a good thing that Brian was away and that only Jesus (and the rats) witnessed the breaking happening within my heart. But now I was in a dilemma. I was deeply aware, I had crossed yet another line in the sand, and I couldn't deny their lives by turning my face away. Every fiber within me wanted to show this film at Colour within our special Sisterhood sessions. I wanted to share this film and I wanted the women to hear this young boy's lament.

To this end I found myself praying, "Father, should I show this? Lord, I don't want to be dramatic...the women come to Colour to be built up and have a good time...Lord, you know we labor hard to make it fun and beautiful...but Lord, this exists...this is terrible...Shall I show it Lord? Is it too much...Will they hear the cry within the cry? Father, I need your wisdom."

Well, I chose to show it. I relinquished one of my own teaching sessions and factored the film in. I sought permission from the filmmakers and I asked the girls gathered that year to sit back and see a part of the world that, for whatever reason, had come crashing into our heart-view. I guess in some ways it was no different from that Thursday morning in Sydney when several hundred of my girls leant into Mende's story and were forever changed. However, this time it was on scale. God knew that seventeen thousand of His girls were about to converge on Sydney, and He knew that if He had his way, seventeen thousand girls would then scatter to the four corners of the earth with a new conviction burning in their hearts.

As the film ended, the vast arena lights slowly brought the gathered girls back into view, and what I encountered was insane—an ocean of faces and emotion staring back at me in silence. The entire stadium was raw with awareness and an instinctive desire to do something. I dismissed the arena for a much-needed emotional coffee (and bladder) break.

During the break, conversation was measured in my back room. All our hearts had been moved in ways hard to describe. One of my team approached and said that some delegates were asking if we were going to receive an offering for this situation.

Something Needs to Be Done

To be honest, I couldn't have agreed more that something needed to be done—but I had a conviction regarding the raising of money and the receiving of offerings at my conference. Colour gathers women from practically every denomination in the Body of Christ, and our chosen ethos is that we will not receive "cause-driven offerings" but will instead create strategies where the girls can return home to their own settings and mobilize response from there.

In this way, I feel we are respecting the vision and mission-giving of the many different churches represented. As a senior pastor, I never want to usurp vision that belongs elsewhere, and as a leader in our own nation my desire is to inspire women to involvement and possibilities in their own churches and communities. But having said that, we do feel that part of our mandate is to create ideas for those lacking in vision or strategy.

So while I was in agreement that we must do something, I was also in a quandary. I hadn't wept in that cabin and then shown this pressing need for no reason. Yet again, a quiet prayer went heavenward; it was a moment to declare complete and utter dependence upon God.

Bobbie, What Are You Doing?

We came back into the next session, where one of my guest speakers was scheduled to teach and a short creative piece was in play before I introduced her. As I sat waiting, a strange thing happened. I suddenly felt compelled to open my purse and take out two fifty-dollar bills. I hurriedly stuffed them down my bra. I think someone along the row looked at me as if to say, *What are you doing?* I had a vague inkling that maybe I should receive a cause-driven offering for Marilyn and the region, but I wasn't exactly sure...When in doubt, trust and *obey*.

After my guest had spoken, I addressed the women. "So, girls, regarding the film we just saw, do you think we should help?" I could see girls nodding in agreement. I then said, "So do you think we should receive an offering?" I'd never done this before, but maybe this need demanded an exception. Surely we couldn't stand by, observe this despair, hear that cry, and not respond—the faces of those staring at me were obviously keen.

"Okay, let's prepare something. Everyone, if you can and if you want, prepare an offering." I pulled out the cash I had stashed down my bra, and then in all honesty God completely took over. I'm seriously not clever enough to have preconceived this moment—it was the strategic direction and urging of His Spirit. I stood there with my dollar bills scrunched in my hand and said:

"Okay, girls...do you have something to give?"
"Yes" was the overwhelming response.
"So, girls...what you are offering is for this need, right?"
"Yes!"
"So, what's in your hand, it's an offering. You're giving it, right?"
"Yes, Bobbie!" I could see them leaning forward as if to say, *What is she doing? Why is she repeating the question?*

"So again, girls...what's in your hand is for these children, this
    need? It's not yours, you're giving it?"
"Yes, yes, yes, Bobbie!!!"
"Okay, here's the deal...I'm not receiving it!"

Whoa. You could have heard a pin drop. "I'm *not* receiving
it, girls...Many of you are desperate to make a difference in the
world...You are desperate to help...but some of you feel so incapable. You feel like you have so little in your hand to offer...Well,
we're not receiving this offering because God is giving this back to
you *as seed to grow*."

Oh my goodness—in that split second of God-only genius, seventeen thousand feminine hearts were suddenly empowered with a
choice and a challenge from above. It was as though the Lord said,
"Okay, my darlings. Here is seed, go grow it into something totally
miraculous."

In retrospect, I think some may have fainted on the spot—it
was a daunting suggestion. For some, it may have been easier to
pop something into the offering container that day and feel—
correctly—that they had contributed to a pressing need. And if
they had done that, it would have been noble and beautiful, but
Father God was after more. He was seeking not merely to gather
and equip, He was seeking to mobilize His daughters into a force—
a force that most of us didn't have a clue we could be, a force also
that would facilitate confidence and personal fulfillment. I was
intentionally pedantic (and repetitive) about what they held in
their hand, because it was actually commissioned money they were
now tucking back into their wallets or purses (or bras).

What transpired is that many—not all, of course, but many—
walked away from the day and took up the challenge. I know of girls
who put their thinking caps on, gathered their friends, and grew
their seed into amounts they never would have imagined possible.

Four Anglican housewives sat on the floor in the arena hallway after that session. They had no idea what they could do, but they were willing to give it a shot. One of them, Megan, told me she had fifty dollars in her hand and would have been content to give it. She and her friends, however, went on to rally their husbands, their church, and their world of influence—they hosted a gala function and grew their seed into a miraculous $120,000.

Another young girl in the ocean of seventeen thousand faces went home to America. She shared the need with her pastor, who then rallied his church to get on board. That church went on to donate $100,000 to the work of helping these children and the people in that region. The stories are many and varied, and I feel it not inappropriate to say that possibly millions of dollars were raised because God's Spirit laid out a challenge and, more importantly, a strategy.

The miracle is definitely that a wave of financial response enabled Watoto to make huge inroads into northern Uganda, but the greater miracle is perhaps what happened in the hearts of willing women who allowed their lives and capacity to be stretched. We were in some ways lovingly tricked by the Spirit of God into discovering there is more within us than we realize—many of us had talents, gifts, and entrepreneurial skills that lay untapped till that year. Years down the track, He lovingly tricked us again with coins and a little lime-colored tin—but I'll save that story for another time.

Be Encouraged

What transpired in what we affectionately now call "the cleavage offering" is one of the sweetest memories and a testimony to what God's girls can accomplish with just a little bit of encouragement. Proverbs 31 speaks of an entrepreneurial woman who observes new fields and then applies her hand. What was becoming remarkably obvious is that the genius of God, plus an ear to His direction and leading, is indeed capable of fantastic things. I will confess that when I dismissed the venue for a morning tea break, I sat down on the edge of the stage trembling—the rats and rebels, intercession, and sleepless nights had all been for a purpose.

I often say to our team that it is not simply about applying good ideas to the cause at hand, because the world is full of good ideas. Good ideas often work, but what we need are the "God ideas"—the divinely inspired strategies that enable strategic inroads into His purposes. God has strategies for all of us, strategies in our personal lives and strategies for the harvest at hand.

I want to encourage you personally.

Your personal challenges are as important as the challenge of the killing fields of northern Uganda or anywhere else in the world. As much as God has strategies of intervention and rescue for the beloved orphans and victims in Uganda, He also has strategies of intervention and rescue for you. Your marriage or family situation is important to Him; your career challenge or health issue is not on the bottom shelf of importance. I want to encourage you to turn your heart and ear heavenward and believe that God's Spirit is well able to help you. If you haven't opened the Word for a while, open it and trust Him to give you direction.

Those of you who were around for the "cleavage challenge" will remember these years with affection. If you and your friends turned your seed into something more, well done and congratulations—and if you didn't, there is honestly no condemnation. We're all in this together, and the most important thing is that God is always trying to teach us that there is more within us than we realize.

That year, rats in a tin-shed cabin and rebels in a faraway land colored my own personal reality. As a Sisterhood, we were only just entering the war zone of northern Uganda, and many of us were about to experience things that were a far cry from our everyday lives, but in the exposure to such things lay a ripple effect of fruitfulness... hundredfold fruitfulness if God could have His way.

Stampeding stilettos still awaited us, as did other fields, other war zones, and a myriad of other miraculous stories.

seventeen

MY SISTER'S KEEPER

(The Response)

*B*obbie...*women are STAMPEDING to the marquee... They're literally climbing over each other!"*

Well, I'm sure there was a tiny bit of embellishment in that joyful statement by a longtime girlfriend, but women were apparently racing each other to the big white tent on the forecourt of the arena to step into the fray and "adopt a sister!" In a matter of moments, one thousand perfectly and beautifully displayed profiles of sisters in need had been snapped up, with girls exclaiming, "I want a sister! Are there more? Surely we have more!"

Such is the nature of empathy unleashed and true Sisterhood unharnessed. Such was a moment that surely had the Father smiling in affectionate pride—His girls were getting it. They were beginning to truly understand and were stoically looking beyond their own issues and complexities to become the fabulous Sisterhood He had in mind before the foundations of the earth. The moment didn't mean that the girls in the race to the tent were suddenly without their own challenges, but it is remarkable how our own circumstances pale into finer perspective when we are confronted with the extreme plight of others.

"Goodness, maybe *the world hasn't ended* because my state-of-the-art washing machine just broke."

"Wow, maybe I should be grateful that I have kids who can play sport and enjoy dance lessons—maybe driving them here, there, and everywhere isn't the burden I make it out to be."

"Yeah—maybe my husband's devotion to work and calling isn't the enemy I too often turn it into."

Perspective is a fabulous reality check. It has the ability to ground us and make us ever so thankful for the blessings we do have. Perspective is when God arrests your attention, draws you to higher ground, and more or less says, "Okay, honey, have a good look at the world. No matter what may have happened to you, no matter what you might be experiencing right now, there is always someone worse off—so let's take a deep breath and give attention and energy to what's really important."

I am in no way diminishing the challenges of life. Whether the nation we live in is categorized as "developed" or "developing" isn't the issue—brokenness is brokenness, abandonment is abandonment, abuse is abuse. And tragically, these (and many more conditions) assail the human soul regardless of background, culture, or status. All are painful and none are what God intended for any of us. It is indeed a broken world that so often reproduces brokenness—and lest we ever forget, this is the very reason Jesus Christ came.

Profiles and Perspective

The profiles in the big white tent were of Ugandan sisters primarily suffering from HIV/AIDS. This virus was vehemently out of control throughout all of Africa as well as other parts of the world. It was rapidly robbing families of parents, and if something dramatic didn't happen to turn back the tidal wave of death, it was suggested that by 2010 an estimated fifty million children would become orphans in Africa alone.

Our beloved friends the Skinners had been inspired to start their original ministry to children because years before Gary had encountered an elderly grandmother who was caring for her twenty-six grandchildren alone. Her own adult children had died of the disease and here was a dear woman in her latter years, fending for a tribe of young, energetic, and needy grandchildren. She told Gary that she was too old to dig—too old to dig for food, too old to dig for survival.

It was in that moment of stark reality that Gary Skinner heard again the cry of the afflicted and felt God challenge him not only to look after this woman's children but to realize that they were actually His children. The orphaned infant, child, and teenager were important to God—they were His and someone needed to step into the challenge because, after all, true religion is described in the book of James as caring for the widow and orphan in their distress: "Religion that God our Father accepts as pure and faultless is this: to look after orphans and widows in their distress and to keep oneself from being polluted by the world" (James 1:27).

I don't pretend to be an expert on this subject, but most would agree that the situation needed to be addressed from all angles. World organizations were awakening, the celebrity world was awakening, and government bodies were awakening. The church, with her vast resource of people, also needed to awaken.

Cafés and Girlfriends

And so it was in a bustling London café that Marilyn, Cathy Clarke (our Hillsong London pastor), and I had a conversation. In the midst of some good old-fashioned fellowship, we agreed to an idea that was embryonic:

• The Skinners' church in Kampala had a strong, flourishing, and caring congregation with hundreds of "connect groups" in nearly every community of the city.

• Antiretroviral drugs had become more affordable and accessible in Africa, and the Skinners had conceived a plan of response that would ask every connect group to be watchful for any woman in their respective neighborhoods who might have HIV/AIDS. It didn't matter if they were part of their church or not; it didn't matter if they were Christian or atheist, Muslim, or of any other faith— what mattered was that they were suffering and in need of care.

• Their strategy and hope was that, through genuine relationship, each connect group could locate a woman and family in need and extend the offer to help her receive and administer the antiviral medication.

Helping a woman receive and administer these drugs is more complicated than many of us may realize—it's not quite as simple as a prognosis and a visit to the local clinic. With the diagnosis of HIV/AIDS can come extreme stigma, rejection, and persecution. If a woman has the virus, she can be thrown out of her home. Her husband (even if he is the source of infection) can confiscate everything. An HIV-positive woman is often branded untouchable in society, left alone to fend for herself with no support, family, or means. The administration of the drugs is also critical. If the drugs are given in time, correctly, and consistently, she will live. The Skinners knew that the only hope for many of these vulnerable women would be the kindness and grace of God in and through a caring congregation who would come alongside and pass no judgment.

As we sat in the London café listening to Marilyn describe the beginnings of this initiative, Cathy and I leaned in again and said, "Mar, if we as a church can help, if we as a Sisterhood can help in any way, we're here for you, babe." It was from here that the divine wheels of motion yet again went into a flurry of action.

Marilyn returned home to Uganda and mobilized her ever-faithful team to start finding and profiling these dear vulnerable women, not only in Kampala but also in Gulu, northern Uganda. The strategy was not dissimilar to child sponsorship:

- Find a woman in need.
- Ascertain if she wants help and allay her fears.
- Profile her life as much as possible.
- Register her into this new program.
- Find sisters around the world willing to commit and sponsor the cost of her monthly antiretroviral drugs.
- Provide training in livelihood creation and literacy, as well as food and practical support.

In other words, we the Sisterhood will sponsor her drugs and the church in Kampala will facilitate the human touch and connection in the administration of her medical rescue.

At the time, none of us truly knew where this would lead.

Returning Captives

March arrived and we launched this new and exciting program. I recall a comment from another girlfriend who oversees a massive aid and relief portfolio in a renowned world organization. She said to me, "Bobbie, this is potentially brilliant. Organizations like ours are hampered on the borders because corruption and complexity so often sabotage the delivery process. This strategy to get the drugs where they need to be, effectively and efficiently, is awesome."

And so it was for these lovingly gathered and laboriously administered profiles that our Colour girls were stampeding to the marquee.

Marilyn's team had initially sourced one thousand women in need of immediate intervention. I have to say again that it wasn't an easy process for the Kampala team to execute. Because of the stigma, many women don't want it known that they are HIV positive, so the process had to be undertaken with wisdom, grace, and sensitivity. Pioneering any noble endeavor has to start somewhere—and then as the process unfolds, it develops into what it ultimately needs to be.

As I write of these early days, Marilyn reminds me that word got out in Gulu that Watoto was offering help. As already said, this region was in the harsh aftermath of civil war, and the challenges were complex. The rebel forces still existed, but certain breakthroughs were happening. Many previously abducted children—now older and with children of their own from their captivity—were returning from the bush to the towns from which they were taken captive, and the large refugee camps that had protected hundreds of thousands of traumatized people were also being dismantled. One would think that all returning captives would be welcomed home (yellow ribbons around the trees, right?), but sadly the severity of war carried stigma for them also. Instead of welcome, many were met with rejection and persecution from the people who had previously been their family and community.

So as word of the coming aid spread, ten thousand vulnerable women turned up for help. *Ten thousand!* At this point, our friends only had the capacity to help one thousand. Marilyn told me that one of the hardest days in her thirty-year missionary life was the day she had to tell nine thousand desperate and hopeful women that she didn't have the means to help them at this stage—it was heartbreaking, to say the least.

I don't know how you, dear friend, would handle this, but I know I would want to fall apart on the spot. I deeply empathize as I watch humanitarian aid trying to deal with the immensity of today's global disasters and problems. Naturally we could all become overwhelmed and draw back, but how many of us know that this isn't the answer? The only way to clean up a mess is to start somewhere.

Our attitude and mantra in our church is: "We can't do everything, but we must do something." If we all just started with what is in our hand, the miraculous would take place.

They Don't Have to Die

In our Sisterhood sessions that year (2008, one year after we had heard the cry of Jacob), we took what was in our hand and excitedly and tentatively presented this new initiative called Living Hope. Marilyn wanted these vulnerable women to know there was living, real, felt, heaven-sent hope! If the drugs were administered correctly, the women would not die—and if they didn't die, their children would not be added to the tragedy of rapidly escalating orphan statistics.

I can't tell you how encouraging it was to hear and see the response of the Sisterhood that morning at Colour. Stilettos or not, those able and keen had run as fast as their little feet would carry them to the marquee. I wish I'd seen it firsthand, and I wish I'd had a film crew out there on the forecourt to capture it all—but we had had no idea if women would stretch again to yet another pressing need, and in many ways we had prepared the marquee and the profiles in faith.

Yet within that glorious moment, sisters in the Sydney conference had stepped bravely, passionately, and enthusiastically into the need and plight of sisters in a faraway land. Sisterhood was in full motion, and as I write this, I want to cry again at the goodness of God. His Word declares as beautiful the feet of those who run with good news: "*How beautiful* on the mountains are the feet of the messenger bringing good news, breaking the news that all's well, proclaiming good times, announcing salvation, telling Zion, 'Your God reigns!' Voices! Listen!...GOD has rolled up his sleeves. All the nations can see his holy, muscled arm. Everyone, from one end of the earth to the other, sees him at work, doing his salvation work" (Isa. 52:7–10 MSG, emphasis mine).

To a broken and rejected woman, how beautiful the news must be that she is *not* forgotten or condemned to a lonely existence or death. How soul-replenishing to know that someone cares and that someone has a plan for your survival—that a faraway someone, a faraway sister, a faraway Sisterhood in a world so removed from yours has chosen to roll up their sleeves, flex their strength, and bring whatever offering or aid they have to the table. Indeed, how beautiful are the feet of those who run full pelt to a marquee tent to adopt a sister in need.

Imagine

From the perspective of these African sisters, we can only imagine the joy and relief when they were told that someone had adopted them—yet "imagine" is exactly what God has asked us to do. In the early years of Colour, the vision was also framed with the statement: "If one woman can change her world, imagine what one company of women can do!"

As you have probably gathered, I love the example of Mother Teresa. She was one woman who radically changed the world—and if she could, then why couldn't we? She was an astounding woman whose kindness affected multitudes, but as we know, she had passed, and while her legacy and inspiration will forever remain, it was now our turn. The baton had passed and we needed to be part of a new generation willing to care and step into the fray. As I remember this story, I now know how brilliant women are when awakened and mobilized. I now know that together we can make a difference. And I now know that when women are truly united in friendship and cause, we can become that force spoken of in the Bible.

The girls were now not merely a movement of world changers in theory (or in faith). We were fast becoming a movement of world changers in *motion*. In the months following, as the Living Hope strategy unfolded and became reality for many (including many more of the nine thousand turned away in Gulu), I found myself again on Ugandan soil. I had a film crew with me this time, because I wanted to bring the story home to the girls at Colour.

Sissy

The Kampala team had arranged for us to meet Sissy. Her story is somewhat crazy. I think it will make you gasp and then smile in a way that incites belief that goodness still prevails in an often hostile, unfair world.

The local connect group had heard that there was a woman suffering in the community. She had been diagnosed with HIV/AIDS, had been thrown out of her family, and was homeless and helpless. The disease was taking its advanced toll on her body. I've never personally seen the extreme effects of HIV/AIDS, but in her case, her flesh was literally starting to deteriorate and rot, and the rats were starting to eat her flesh as she slept wherever she could. Take a moment to digest that information. Sissy would take uninvited shelter on the verandas of different homes in the neighborhood, and apparently many would shoo her away because they didn't want a broken, diseased woman on their doorstep.

But the church found her.

Thank God for the church. Critics often diminish the worth of the church in modern society, yet if intelligent analysis were made in most cities and towns around the world, you'd find that it is often the church that voluntarily administers enormous social welfare, saving local and federal governments millions of dollars. So, long story short, the church intervened. Sissy was befriended and embraced, and started on her treatment. When I met her, she had responded miraculously. Her body had recovered and her skin was healed and glowing. She had also leaned into the love of God and had opened her heart to Jesus, making Him Lord of her life. Her transformation was stunning, and she was hilarious!

As we gathered in the lovely home of her personal connect leader and squished too many bodies—including the film crew— into the living room, Sissy couldn't wait to share her story and give glory to God. She had the whitest teeth on the planet and a smile to die for—and to be honest, we probably used a truckload of film rolls because the girl basically wouldn't stop talking. She was delightfully full of gratitude, praise, and vision, not only for her own life, but also for that of others.

She later took us to visit her own home. We followed her down a dusty alley not far from the leader's home, where she proudly opened the door to a simple space, maybe no larger than ten feet by ten feet. She had a mattress and a few minimal belongings. Despite a raw and dusty floor, it was clean and perfect. I quietly looked up at the tin ceiling and tucked into a small crevice was her toothbrush. With my friends, I thanked her for graciously sharing her world and her home.

Two-Way Street

Her literal dwelling place may have been sparse, but the dwelling place of her heart and true personhood was overflowing with the exceeding and abundant goodness of God (see Eph. 3:20 KJV). She was full of joy unspeakable. Our visit had been both inspiring and humbling, and I pray that her life is going from strength to strength.

Sissy is one of many, many sisters whom heaven had chosen to bring into our lives—but the power of Sisterhood isn't only a one-way street.

What we were to discover is that this rapidly emerging African Sisterhood would also profoundly bless us. God had knit our lives together for reasons beyond our initial knowing: Their beautiful lives would be helped by us, but relationship is a fabulous two-way street, and in all seriousness, our lives would be deeply inspired and helped by them. Their examples of courage, bravery, endurance, grace, forgiveness, and sheer overcoming spirit would become a force and catalyst for what God had prepared for us down the road.

Local and Global

I'm confident we will all agree that the human heart is in need of help everywhere, and the power of Sisterhood is intrinsically both local and global. It's not one or the other, it's both, and I believe God wants us to give attention and due diligence to both. For some, the glamour of faraway foreign fields beclouds the equal wonder of what sits beneath our noses. The miracle of response is closer than many realize, often no farther than across the back fence or down the very streets we live on. Our own local "hood" and the people we do everyday life with are as important as pressing global needs.

The Living Hope program was actually a local response from a local church in Africa. To me, Africa is completely global—it's a faraway exotic land, full of what I would call compelling global need—but to Marilyn and her congregation, it's completely local. We each have a critical local community to be mindful of and responsible for, yet it is amazing how the lines can blur in this context.

Right and Wrong

Changing the world is one big learning curve. The Great Commission and all it entails is of paramount importance—it can't be neglected. It's why the church actually exists, but there are also right and wrong ways to go about it.

God certainly wants to enlarge our capacity to reach and help others, but never at the expense of our own vineyard, home, family, and planting (the local of all our lives). When the early disciples were being commissioned to go reach their world, a certain order of priority was given to them: "You will be my witnesses in Jerusalem, and in all Judea and Samaria, and to the ends of the earth" (Acts 1:8). Sometimes we want to start with the "ends of the earth" and work backward, when God wants us to take care of what is in our immediate sphere and then work from there. Do that with integrity and faithfulness, and it's amazing how the rest of what may be in your heart to achieve will follow. My husband teaches this perfectly in his book *Live Love Lead*, explaining the principle of taking what is in your hand to fulfill what is in your heart.

The remarkable, caring, and entrepreneurial Proverbs 31 woman had it in perfect perspective. Of her the Bible says, "She considers a [new] field before she buys or accepts it [expanding prudently and not courting neglect of her present duties by assuming other duties]; with her savings [of time and strength] she plants fruitful vines in her vineyard" (Prov. 31:16 AMP, emphasis mine).

Around this period, I received a letter from a husband. I read it and quietly heard the lament of his heart. He was genuinely happy for his wife to be inspired to make the world a better place, but he was simply asking that in the midst of all the exciting global endeavor, could we please not fail to be mindful of home. His tone wasn't nasty or judgmental—he just wanted me to be mindful of something. His beloved wife had become so obsessed with foreign fields that attention to their own home, household, marriage, and family was being overlooked. With utmost care and discretion, I relayed the spirit of his letter and concern to the conference, with the hope that we would all wisely take on board the spirit of the reminder.

Maturity and Correction

It was into all these realities and more that we were maturing. Growing in stature and authority and being able to effectively influence the world is a process—a glorious process that isn't afraid of both direction and correction.

One is a little more glamorous than the other. We like the idea of godly direction leading us into wide, open, and exciting places, but are we as warm to the idea of godly correction keeping us safe in those wide, open, exciting places? If we as followers and fellow laborers with Him aren't open to correction on any number of personal levels, then it's unlikely that God will actually allow us to graduate to more expansive places.

Truth at any level of life ultimately leads to freedom and liberty—and freedom and liberty are what this entire message is about. Therefore, I want to encourage us all to be ever open to the Spirit of God in our lives. The Bible says that the Holy Spirit is our Helper. Jesus describes Him as the Spirit of Truth who leads us into all truth—so if God's Spirit puts His finger on an aspect of your heart or character, allow Him to do so. Our response to His hand upon our life is as important as our ability to respond to the humanitarian needs within this greater story. He knows way more than we, and He knows what has the capacity to bless us, hurt us, or take us out.

The magnitude of becoming our sisters' keepers wasn't small or insignificant. It actually involved millions of lives in desperate need, and it would demand a purity of heart and a willingness to be teachable. Turn the page with me and let's take a little stroll through some ancient fields in ancient history.

eighteen

WHERE ARE THEY?

(The Fields)

Have you ever lost someone and been desperate to find them? When Brian and I were first engaged, we bought a dog—a gorgeous golden retriever pup called Kelly. I had wanted a dog all my life but for some reason wasn't allowed one, so I was absolutely besotted. One day, I walked him to the local shops, tied him carefully to a trash can, and popped inside the store. Suddenly, a car loudly backfired. I swung around to see my new baby bolt. I dropped everything and ran outside, but all that could be seen was a twelve-week-old ball of white fluff disappearing at high speed down the road, trash can still attached and flailing wildly behind him.

All night we searched the streets, and I even posted a lost-puppy announcement on the radio. We eventually found him the next day. He had hightailed it home (clever puppy) but had taken one street too early (bless him) and had been sitting in a driveway the equivalent distance down the road to my house.

Loss

I lost my son Joel once. He's impossible to lose now because he's *Avatar* tall and stands out in any crowd, but on this occasion he

wasn't yet three. I lost him at the airport for a good forty-five min-
utes, which is an eternity to any young mom. I had airport security and staff searching everywhere. What was most disconcerting
was that the airport was almost empty and he was nowhere to be
found—the worst thoughts of abduction went through my mind.
As I kissed my worried mother good-bye because her flight was
leaving, I found a public phone booth and dragged Ben's stroller as
far into the booth as I could. With one hand on the stroller and the
other searching for coins, I called Brian. "Honey, I don't know how
to tell you this, but Joel's lost...like seriously lost...We can't find
him anywhere, everyone is looking."

Brian was calm (he's always calm in a crisis) and said he would
come. I walked back into the vast empty departure area trying to
hold back emotion and stay composed—and then suddenly, from
nowhere, I saw a tall, stately flight captain coming toward me with
my little boy happily holding his hand. Who knows where and how
far he had wandered, but it had taken an army of airport personnel
almost an hour to find him.

My worst loss was my father. He died suddenly when I was fourteen. The unbearable part was the overwhelming sense of separation from a man I adored with all my being. It felt like my broken,
hemorrhaging heart would never mend—it did, but that's also
another story.

I'm sure you can relate to loss somewhere in your life. It's almost
impossible to be human and not experience loss at some point in
the journey.

I actually have a theory about loss, grief, and pain. I believe we
are not created or wired for any of it. I believe God created us for a
perfect environment, a garden of everlasting relationship, love, and
goodness. Of course, we know the Genesis fall messed that up,
and with time and distance we've learned to compensate and survive. However, being lost and feeling loss isn't how God intended

existence, hence the naming of this chapter. Four chapters into the greatest love story of all time, the Bible, God's first family experienced loss and were perhaps asking the same question that I'm presenting: "*Where are they?*"

Something Is Not Right

"Adam, have you seen the boys? Adam, where are they? Something is not right."

I know Eve went on to have other children, but at this juncture in ancient history, only two sons are recorded. Like Eve, I also have two sons. Mine are all grown and not likely to lose themselves in airports anymore. They're now husbands and fathers (and ministers, for that matter), but they still love boyish adventure. Given half the chance, they'll throw caution to the wind and take off to crazy locations to surf the insane waves of Indonesia and get themselves into all sorts of drama. If it wasn't for certain social media, I'd have no clue where my boys are or what they're up to. I'm not really complaining. They're fabulous adults, their lives are actually theirs to manage and mastermind, and their mother doesn't always need to know, but I do empathize with the question that mothers the world over (including Eve) often ask: "Where are the boys?"

The early pages of Genesis don't paint an overly detailed account of that notable day when Cain murdered Abel, so we're going to have to use imagination here, but I daresay God wasn't the only one asking the question about Abel's whereabouts. Their parents must have sensed that something was wrong.

Centuries on, it's easy to make judgments about Adam and Eve, but (hello) we weren't actually there. The insanely perfect setting of Eden had been brutally interrupted by independence, disobedience, and consequence, and this first-ever family had been plunged into the catastrophic fallout. Personally, I believe Eve found grace, and I'm hoping to sit with her one day in eternity under a shady tree and ask exactly how it was to be among the first of all creation. She was to bear the consequence of her decision in no uncertain terms, but her husband (equally responsible) went on to name her "the mother of all the living" (Gen. 3:20). God personally came down and sewed coverings of animal skin for them (see Gen. 3:21). Had He not loved them, He would not have done that. Had He not still believed in them, He would have totally abandoned them. Yes, they were walking in the severe consequence of choice, yet they remained His beloved son and daughter, and His relentless love was not going to fail them.

Entering the frame, we now have two beautiful baby boys.

I can only imagine that they were gorgeous. "Gorgeous" isn't exactly a Bible word, but bear with my imagination. The Bible says that they grew and then one day went out into the fields. Where were they? I'll surmise that they probably weren't playing a friendly game of hide and seek. They were young men who had chosen career paths in farming—one a herdsman, the other a man of the soil. Genesis 4 recounts events like this:

> Adam made love to his wife Eve, and she became pregnant and gave birth to Cain. She said, "With the help of the LORD I have brought forth a man." Later she gave birth to his brother Abel.
>
> Now Abel kept flocks, and Cain worked the soil. In the course of time Cain brought some of the fruits of the soil as an offering to the LORD. And Abel also brought an offering—fat portions from some of the firstborn of his flock. The LORD looked with favor on Abel and his offering, but on Cain and his offering he did not look with favor. So Cain was very angry, and his face was downcast.

Then the LORD said to Cain, "Why are you angry? Why is your face downcast? If you do what is right, will you not be accepted? But if you do not do what is right, sin is crouching at your door; it desires to have you, but you must rule over it."

Now Cain said to his brother Abel, "Let's go out to the field." While they were in the field, Cain attacked his brother Abel and killed him.

Then the LORD said to Cain, *"Where is your brother Abel?"*

"I don't know," he replied. "Am I my brother's keeper?"

The LORD said, "What have you done? Listen! Your brother's blood cries out to me from the ground." (Genesis 4:1–10, emphasis mine)

Intrigue and Tragedy in the Field

Tragically, what had happened in the field was sinister. Sin had indeed crouched at the door of Cain's heart and had not been resisted or governed. The consequence was violence—violence against a brother.

I find God's questions intriguing. Surely God knows all and nothing is hidden from His sight, yet He still asks Cain the question about his brother's whereabouts. The guilty Cain responds, "I don't know. Am I my brother's keeper?" Who really knows the tone of the reply? Who knows if attitude, arrogance, guilt, or shame were within his words? The Bible doesn't really say, but I have to wonder if the tone wasn't somewhat rebellious. Envy, independence, and sin had taken residence in Cain's heart, and with such will often come contempt for what is right and of importance to God.

There are several lessons in the story: that of first fruits, that of honor, and that of being teachable. In all truthfulness, God was simply parenting Cain with a valuable lesson about what was right and what was wrong, but whatever was brewing under the surface of Cain's heart had already given way to treachery and tragedy. The haunting question now focused on the well-being of the younger brother: "Where is your brother Abel?" Cain replies, and then God says, "What have you done? Listen! Your brother's blood cries out to me from the ground."

The Sobering Question Still Applies

When I read these verses a few years ago, I felt God's Spirit quicken them in context of the Sisterhood. The gender changed, of course, but the principle was the same. I saw this same question in the light of you and me entering the gates of heaven. Can you imagine the wonder of that day? Then suddenly, somewhere in the mix of all the wide-eyed excitement, welcome, and celebration, the Lord asks, "So, where is your sister?"

"Where is she, Bobbie?
"Christine...where is she?
"Laura, Donna, Carol, Amanda...where are they?
"Sweetheart, where is your sister?"

Imagine the Lord asking you that question. Of course, I'm painting a broad hypothetical here, but it's a hypothetical with truth. It doesn't matter if you have a literal sister or not. The question relates to the fact that the human race is one giant global family and therefore we have responsibility toward one another, especially when it is within our power to influence positively. And in that context, the question could well be asked of us. The sister, the friend, the mother, the neighbor, the woman we rub shoulders with in our everyday existence—where is she? Did we befriend her or embrace her? Did we listen to her? When she was suffering, were we there to offer support? This gospel that we hold so dear, did we ever share it with her? The sister in captivity and slavery, the one who cries out to a God she is unsure even exists, the one who is so desperate for prayer to prevail on her behalf—did we pray, did we remember her? Where is the one whom you were purposed and assigned to bring hand in hand into His presence, paradise, kingdom, and freedom?

I hope the Father never looks at any one of us and says the words he said to Cain: "Daughter, what have you done (*or not done*)? Listen! Her blood cries out to me from the ground."

As I pen these words, I don't mean to cast shadow or guilt over this beautiful uplifting Sisterhood story. If we're all honest, we've all had moments of lost opportunity with people. I recall many years ago seeing a woman crying in the local mall. I honestly think I may have walked past her several times, concerned for her sorrow but lacking the courage to inquire after her well-being. Now, all these years on, if I saw her I would have no hesitation in gently asking if she was okay, but back then I lacked the courage to interfere and intervene. Sometimes our fear of interfering clouds God's intent for us to graciously intervene and, more often than not, be involved in a life-changing miracle.

I'm not talking about the lost opportunities we can't redeem—if a lost moment comes to mind, quietly commit that person to prayer and trust that God will put plan B into action. What I am challenging is the reality of *now* and what lies ahead. I wonder if in this enlightened, resourced, enabled, and different day, God isn't asking—and expecting—more of us because he knows there is more within us.

Cain challenged God with his question about being his brother's keeper. I don't believe that we are responsible for the entire world, but this current world is on our watch and I do believe we are in a season of church history like no other. Our ability to be aware, bring hope, and ultimately become humanity's keeper in a positive, redemptive way is unprecedented.

The Fields

Fields are part of the landscape of the days ahead, and therefore they are part of the landscape of the Sisterhood. I don't know what you think of when it comes to fields, but for me different scenarios come to mind.

"Summer fields" bring green grass to mind. I have a quiet love affair with lying on succulent green grass, perhaps because I often mowed the lawns every weekend as a young girl and the smell of cut grass brings with it a flood of childhood memories. Psalm 23 is never far from my thinking—quiet pastures, still waters, summer breeze, and eyes focused heavenward. Perfection.

When I think of fields, the vineyards of Proverbs 31 come to mind. Again, I love how this woman had the capacity to contemplate wisely the fields she will engage and labor within.

And of course, harvest fields and mission fields come to mind, right? Jesus told us to pray laborers into the harvest because the fields are ripe unto harvest (see Luke 10:2). They were ripe in his day, even more so today. Always hold affection and respect for those who faithfully serve in distant mission fields, often sacrificing much for the well-being of others, and often working under difficult conditions.

But the fields that concern my heart in this part of our story are the ones that people were never designed to experience: the "killing fields" that come with war and unrest; the fields that are fraught with danger for vulnerable and oftentimes foolish young people; the ones that seduce our children with enticements that end in despair; the fields where the predator lays ambush and carries away the innocent and unsuspecting, where sin and evil crouch, waiting to devour like a lion in pursuit (see Ps. 10).

Forgive me if this has become momentarily intense, but it was to such a field that Cain and Abel were lured, a field that further ensnared the brother who was not guarding his heart, and a field that ended in bloodshed for the other—a field that ultimately brought despair to all and prompted the probing question: *Where is your brother?*

We live in a world where people are playing and dabbling in fields they were never destined for, fields that are darkening and intensifying in danger and that, without intervention, will be their undoing and demise.

God Lost Us

As salt and light of the earth, we need to be aware of and willing to step into the fray and darkness and go in search of those who are lost. I opened this chapter asking if you have ever lost someone. Well, God lost us—and not because He was distracted or negligent. Sin crouched at the door of Adam and Eve, and then not long after, at the door of their sons. The devil-enemy is intent on us being lost to the Father for all eternity, but as we know, God's plan will always trump the enemy's plan. While we were lost from Eden for a season, we shall one day return to it. With the passage and process of time, God's redemption plan came into play. He sent His Son Jesus Christ to seek, rescue, and restore.

You and I are here now in the continuing process of time with the same mandate and commission. Hopefully we, as the Church of Jesus Christ, are asking the same questions as heaven: Where are they? Are they aware they're lost? Are they aware they're playing in fields that harbor danger? Are they aware this isn't a game? Do they even care?

This Sisterhood message, mandate, movement (call it what you will) is not a "happy-clappy" stroll in the park with a few girlfriends. It's way more than a women's event with lights and streamers. It is about the redemption of heaven's lost sons and daughters. God may not hold us accountable for every man, woman, and child on the planet, but He may well ask the question about those who were under our nose and within the realm of our influence. I believe the Father is challenging us because He knows we are capable of more in this context. The Sisterhood story is proof of that.

Relentless and Endless

My son Joel (with another young man, Matt Crocker) wrote a song called "Relentless." In their words, it became the entry point to the acclaimed Hillsong United album *Zion*. It speaks of God's relentless love.

> *Salvation sounds a new beginning*
> *As distant hearts begin believing*
> *Redemption's bid is unrelenting . . .*
> *Tearing through the veil of darkness*
> *Breaking every chain, You set us free*
> *Fighting for the furthest heart*
> *You gave Your life*
> *Your love is relentless*
> MATT CROCKER AND JOEL
> HOUSTON, "RELENTLESS," 2014

"Fighting for the furthest heart" is the challenge. Remaining mindful and caring of those *desperately lost in the farthest and darkest corners of the field*, while managing our everyday and oftentimes blessed lives, is the endless commission before us.

Therefore, my endless prayer is that I will never succumb and accept the fact that darkness and chains exist. My endless prayer is that I will always be true to my here-and-now life, and that the broken and lost will never be far from my thinking. My endless prayer is that I will always view people with kindness and compassion and that, prompted or unprompted, I will take the time to be attentive, engaged, kind, and gracious. My endless prayer is that when God nudges me to pray, *I will.*

Missio Dei

I'm not suggesting for a minute that being our sister's (or brother's) keeper is going to demand of us what we cannot give, but I am suggesting we all need to wake each day with a sense of mission, a sense of timeless *missio Dei*—the mission and sending of God— that understands that we are alive for such a time as this and there is work to be done; that while it is still day, there are kingdom fields to be entered, opportunities to be engaged, and endeavors to be created that move people from "lost" to "found."

Into this mix and mission we have all been called. If you have come the distance with me in this book, it's highly unlikely that God doesn't want you to be a part of this journey. You have been called by name. Like all of us, you may not be perfect—in fact you may be as flawed as they come—but that's not the issue. The issue is that we have brothers and sisters who need us now. For anyone who thinks they are unworthy of involvement, consider a man I once met who had been a rebel warlord in Uganda. He had orchestrated the slaughter and rape of many. But he had found Christ, had found forgiveness, and his life mission is to reverse the damage inflicted upon those who, in essence, had been his victims. When I met this man, I saw anew the redemptive grace and power of Jesus.

God has us all strategically planted in all corners of the earth.

My address is most likely not yours, and vice versa. I don't rub shoulders with the people you rub shoulders with, nor do you rub shoulders with the people in my world. We each have our unique sphere of influence and opportunity, and within the near and far of all these realms are the lost. Where are they? Don't let their blood cry from the ground—let's be the ones who give our best and do our best to track them home to God.

The Song

As I end this chapter and seed you into the next, I am reminded of a profound lesson found in the book of the Song of Songs. The Song of Songs is a poetic feast tucked in the middle of the Bible, written by the ancient and creative King Solomon. It paints a picture not only of marriage between a man and a woman, but also of the love affair between Jesus and His Church, of which all humanity is called to be a part.

It tells the story of how the woman, weary from a day in the fields, has bathed and put herself to rest. She then hears her lover knocking gently on the lattice of her window, beckoning her to arise and come with him. But tired from her labors, she reasons with herself and lingers—how could she rise and soil her feet again? She hesitates. Then, because she actually loves him, she awakens her response—but he has left; he has withdrawn and disappeared into the night. Her heart mourns her missed opportunity to be with him and work with him. She goes in search but cannot find him. She then awakens, for it was all a dream—a dream that teaches her (and us) a haunting lesson about offered opportunity...and missed opportunity.

The Scripture is full of revelation that speaks to us in endless ways. For me, this story speaks of my Savior, whose work in the night season of this age is not done. He comes knocking yet again on the door of her heart, beckoning her to join Him and once again enter the fray with Him. He beckons her to arise and dress and soil her feet yet again for the cause greater than herself—yet she sadly misses the opportunity.

I shared this thought with the Colour girls around 2015. Anyone observing my conference at this time would perhaps have seen only success. Venues around the world were packed and momentum was obvious, but within my spirit I was mindful of familiarity—the unintentional kind that can so easily creep up when we're not looking. Familiarity that can numb and then morph into complacency, that then reasons:

- We're aware.
- We've had our hearts torn open.
- We've heard the cry of the afflicted.
- We've labored in the field.
- And contributed.
- We've made a difference.
- Please don't knock on the door of my heart *again*.
- Please don't ask me to rise again, pray again, contribute again, or bear the burden again.
- Please don't ask me to enter the darkness again.

My prayer is that we will be like the woman in the Song of Songs. Her heart heard her lover calling and she eventually responded, but I pray that our senses won't be dulled by comfort or familiarity, and that we will always respond the minute we hear that first knock or nudge.

When my little guy Joel wandered off in that airport all those years ago, I said that I had no idea where and how far he had wandered. I was just grateful that a flight captain found him and brought him back to me. The truth is that so many of our brothers and sisters have wandered far and wide into places of darkness and danger. They also need a captain to go find them. Jesus Christ is our Captain and He wants us involved in the redemption of His sons and daughters. Let's be their lifeline.

Brian and I searched all night for a twelve-week-old puppy called Kelly. Let's search as long as it takes for those whose value was so immense that it brought the Son of God from heaven to Earth to find us.

On that brutal cross, Jesus cried, "It is finished" (John 19:30). He paid the price and won the battle to reclaim what had been lost... but our work for and on behalf of that victory is far from over.

• nineteen •

RUSSIAN DOLLS AND A SMILE TO DIE FOR

(The Fight for Value and Freedom)

I have zero capacity to grasp new languages, and despite having traveled into eastern Europe for many years now, my embarrassingly small repertoire of Russian words consists mainly of "spasiba," which means "thank you." Needless to say, I am endlessly thankful when I'm there.

Allow me to give you a little history about our connection and love affair with this part of the world, which has become such an integral part of the Sisterhood landscape.

One House, Many Rooms

Our church in Sydney was very young when we launched out and pioneered a church in Ukraine. Our then youth pastor was a young man called Darko Culjak, an Australian with a Croatian background. He was bold and adventurous, with a passion for leading young people to Christ, when he married a young woman and then tragedy hit. Their short-lived marriage dissolved for reasons not needful to share, and from this place of brokenness, Darko expressed a desire to plant a church in Kiev.

This Kiev "room" was our first-ever global church plant. These days we have Hillsong churches all around the world, and the words "one house, many rooms" frame the vision perfectly. If you were to take the analogy of a big beautiful house with many rooms, then (in all simplicity) you have a picture of our church and our life.

Sydney, under the senior leadership of Brian and myself, is the living room, family room, and center of this big wonderful family house, and all the church plants around the world are the rooms thronging with those who call Hillsong home. Our vision isn't to plant churches everywhere, but as God leads and directs, my husband isn't afraid to stretch into these places. Each of these locations is entrusted to carry the heart and soul of our church with integrity and purity, and all have the freedom to reach into their cities with the gospel. In a nutshell, this global house is overflowing with sons and daughters coming to Christ, and we feel like we are living in the promise and fruit of Isaiah 54:

> Enlarge your house; build an addition. Spread out your home, and spare no expense! For you will soon be bursting at the seams. Your descendants will occupy other nations and resettle the ruined cities. (Isaiah 54:2–3 NLT)

At the time of this first endeavor in Kiev, conditions were of course quite different from how we "church plant" now, but these were the pioneering seeds of our entry into this vast expansive region full of history and intrigue.

The Cold War had ended, yet life in this post-Soviet nation wasn't easy for a young missionary, let alone the people. Commodities on supermarket shelves were sparse and the streets were gray and unfriendly, although the people were hopeful of a better future.

I love Ukrainian food but apparently, the only place you could find anything remotely non-Ukrainian in those early years was in a little pizza restaurant on Tarasa Shevchenko Boulevard, next to the "USA One Dollar" shop.

The initial harshness of this lifestyle took its toll, but Darko felt he was there in the call and timing of God. I recall him telling us that the old Soviet-style building where his apartment was didn't turn the heating on until October, regardless of how severe the weather had become. He would sleep smothered in every inch of clothing he owned. The Bible says that those who sow in tears shall surely reap in joy, and that which is sown in tears shall surely reap a harvest (see Ps. 126:5–6). In this context and upon this offering, God began adding a band of hungry souls who would become our beloved Russian-speaking "sem'ya" (family).

When Can We Get Saved?

Into this mix Darko hired a couple of conservatory-trained musicians. He had no praise and worship team yet, so this was actually quite innovative. The young couple would play, then nip outside for a smoke and a vodka—which is actually hilarious if you don't get all superreligious about it. Several weeks or months into this unusual equation, this young couple naively asked, "When can we get saved?" They went on to become an essential element in this story for many years until circumstances took them elsewhere.

The way Colour became part of the Ukrainian landscape was also unconventional. Darko faithfully pastored our church for five years and then, when he felt his time in Ukraine was over, this young couple I just mentioned became our Hillsong Church lead pastors in Kiev. It was during this period that they came to Sydney on a few occasions and realized that the women in their part of the world desperately needed this message relating to value and worth.

I don't know if there was a breakdown in communication or if it was simply "the Russian way" (smile), but they launched Colour in Kiev without exactly asking me, copying what they had seen in Sydney. I had no real issue with this, except to suggest that maybe next time a conversation might be helpful.

The Ukrainian women "leaned in" heart and soul. They were not used to an environment that went to such lengths to make them feel special. The language of "Warrior Princess Daughter" was for royals and czars, not the everyday women and girls in this part of the world. As I write, I have so many fond memories of our Colour adventures in eastern Europe, but space limits me to sharing but a few:

• I will never forget the childlike shock and wonder when the first-ever confetti explosion happened and twelve hundred Ukrainian sisters were drowned in silver confetti.

• I wish you had been with me when our first-ever Ukrainian opener materialized. When God gave me that original glimpse of thousands gathered, I had no idea that beautiful Russian-speaking sisters on the opposite side of the world would be in the mix. Even now, the reality of it all still brings me to my knees, and my prayer is that I will never take for granted the miracle of a world once closed and cut off, now open to the hope found in Christ.

• I wish you'd seen us outgrow the humble theater our church rented and then graduate to the beautiful October Palace. If you saw any of the political unrest in Kiev in early 2014, you may remember a stately, pale-yellow building with white pillars, set on a hill above perfectly manicured flower beds—snipers were on the roof during the crisis, while the hotel we stayed in across the bridge was converted to a triage center.

It seemed so appropriate to host Colour there, albeit for one year only. I'm told that the building, built in 1838, was (among many other things) used in Soviet days as a debutante ballroom for young women. It was officially called the Institute for Noble Maidens. I love that in that particular year, two and a half thousand women from Ukraine and surrounding nations filled that ballroom with a sense of freedom and worship and were then "presented to the world" with a different and noble sense of empowerment.

• I wish you could have seen our raised eyebrows when we realized that the ominous-looking guard assigned to our tiny green-room was not leaving. I know he was just doing his job, but those of us from outside the region were unaccustomed to these strange eyes and ears watching our every move.

• I wish you had been there when I shared statistics that Ukraine officially had the highest volume of human-trafficked girls in the world. I can still see the entire room staring back at me as if I were from Mars. With my interpreter, I paused and gently repeated, "Girls, listen to me... You do realize this, don't you? More girls go missing from Ukraine than anywhere else in the world."

I went back to my hotel room that afternoon pondering the reaction I had received. Truth is often disturbing. The sobering truth was that women in the audience that day were being confronted, perhaps for the first time, with a reality that was difficult to digest. Perhaps, quietly in their hearts, they were thinking about that young girl from the village or that lovely young niece who excitedly went abroad to work and was strangely never heard of again. Sadly, a new reality was dawning, a reality that God knew we would go on to powerfully address.

• I wish you had been there when we handed out special gifts, carried all the way from Australia in our baggage. The babushka mamas (who squeeze the air from your lungs when they hug you) would not stop exclaiming, "We cannot understand why someone in a faraway land has done this for us...We can't understand why they would love us when they don't even know us."

New Soil, Harsh Mind-sets

Breaking open the soil of a land that has been frozen over with a harsh belief system is something that only the Spirit of God can do. It is only God who can bring a smile to the faces of women who believe that life pretty much ends when you get married.

When I first started going to Kiev I was in my early forties. It would endlessly intrigue the gathered women that I wasn't diminishing in vision or energy at this age. The team there had told me that most girls in that part of the world think that life ends at around thirty—find a man, get married, have children, and then it's all downhill from there, body, soul, and spirit. Not only were the words of this Sisterhood message resonating in hearts, but the example of our lives was also telling a (new) story. Russian women are extremely beautiful—the Beatles even wrote a song about that!—but they're not only beautiful; they're smart, intelligent, gifted, and extremely creative too. The arts abound in this part of the world, and yet for many, that same old cloud of oppression had smothered potential, belief, and joy.

I don't pretend to be an expert in Russian history or the fabulous people of eastern Europe. As with all our global campuses around the world, we trust our positioned leaders to help us understand the complexities and lay of the land and what is needed in response. In this context, two stories come to mind—one relates to a security officer at the airport and a deep malady in the land, and the other relates to a young girl I met a few years later in the hallway of a prestigious venue in Kiev.

"Russian Women Do Not Deserve Gift"

The Warrior Princess Daughter revelation had captivated our hearts, and a few of my close friends started a little tradition of gifting the famous heart-tag Tiffany bracelet to girls on special occasions—on one side we would engrave "Royal daughter" and on the other their name. They were beautiful gifts and at one point I seriously felt that Tiffany should be sponsoring us (hello).

I was en route to Kiev for one of our early conferences and, just as we were doing in Sydney, we wanted to gift the delegates with something lovely and memorable. My friend Holly and her girls from Los Angeles had offered to sponsor the gift; they had sourced imitation Tiffany bracelets in downtown Hollywood (of course) and would ship them to Sydney, where a handful of girls accompanying me to Ukraine that year would help me deliver them to our Kiev team. At this time, Ukraine still suffered corruption in matters of mail and shipping, so rather than risk theft, we decided to carry the gifts in our baggage (and of course, declare them on entry).

All was fine and dandy until one of my Aussie gals arrived a day earlier than the rest of us and incorrectly declared them as silver— they weren't silver, they were pretend silver, but nevertheless Ukrainian customs decided to be difficult. They confiscated the plastic bag of bracelets and gave my friend a taste of old-school interrogation. Enter Ukrainian princess on a mission to retrieve!

Our then lead pastor apparently came down to the airport to explain and rescue the situation, but the security officer decided to contend. When she told him that these were simply "a gift from women in America and Australia to the delegates of a women's conference in Kiev," his harsh response was "Russian women do not deserve gift!"

Are you kidding me? I need a sound bite here so that you can hear the accent and callous tone of what was being said. He was unrelenting, and there was no way these gifts were going to be released for the conference. Well, that response was like a red flag to a bull, because my girl decided to dig her heels in and contend also—not so much for the jolly bracelets but rather for the value and worth of women who for too long have been subjected to this harsh prevailing spirit, which was the antithesis of our entire message and mission.

Misogyny Again

Russian women do deserve gifts—as do African women, Australian, and Asian women. As do American and English and Middle Eastern women. As does any woman or girl who draws breath on this planet. How dare that dark spirit of misogyny say that God's daughters in this part of the world are not worthy!

For five hours that morphed into the night, our team contended. The officer and the system were unrelenting. The next day, I flew in from Australia and had a marginal meltdown in the immigration hall—my Ukrainian team were frantically texting us from the other side of the wall, saying "Do not, we repeat, DO NOT say the 900 bracelets you are carrying are silver!" Okay, I have to admit I can't fill in forms under pressure, especially when they're in Russian with the English in size-zero font underneath, and especially when mean-looking security people are hovering over me with menacing faces. Hilarious now that it's a memory.

Long story short, we had the best-ever Colour. Confetti and bright helium balloons adorned the closing moments, when we handed out the bracelets we did have, and the good news (yay) is that prayer prevailed and customs miraculously released the remaining three hundred bracelets one hour before we needed them. I know this is a strange little story, but it tells a greater story regarding the landscape for women in this part of the world.

For too many centuries, eastern European women had been treated as though they have no value—they were just comrades in the scheme of things and there to be used, abused, and discarded if need be. I know this is not true of all, but it was the way of the world for many in that nation. At the time, I had been told that twelve thousand women die every year in Russia from domestic violence. I know Russia has an enormous population, but seriously, twelve thousand lives is an alarming statistic! This part of the world needed to hear that in the economy of heaven women are loved and deeply valued, and secondly that they have a powerful part to play in the emerging Sisterhood story . . . that they also were called to bring a grace-filled redemptive message to that part of the world. For perspective on how important this Sisterhood and value message is, current global stats have put the number of women suffering domestic violence at the *one billion* mark. The planet is indeed not well on a number of fronts.

An Epiphany

The day I declared over the Kiev Colour girls that they too were part of this Sisterhood was an epiphany for all in the room.

For years, our Russian-speaking sisters had found encouragement in knowing that they were not alone and that there were sisters all around the world loving them, praying for them, and cheering them on. However, the day I told them that they also would become this force of good to others in their realm of influence in eastern Europe and beyond, it was as though they literally sat up and leaned forward. It was as if God's Spirit breathed life into those words and became living revelation in their spirit.

Since that day, a marked shift happened in our Colour Kiev girls. They seemed to come of age and realize that they have a huge role to play in this fabulous global message of hope.

Don't underestimate what God wants to do in your life. You're not reading all these words because you've simply stumbled across this book. Who knows whether the next woman or girl you encounter isn't a perfect candidate to hear she is loved and valued and not forgotten? Who knows what drama she needs to be rescued from?

The Smile to Die For

The other moment I want to share was equally powerful. It involved our first-ever rescued victim of human trafficking and her first words to me, which I will never forget.

Our response to trafficking had already begun, because of that article I had read on a Sunday afternoon about the twenty-seven million involved in modern-day slavery. At the time, none of us knew exactly how to respond. My friend Christine was passionate about the issue, and somewhere in a random conversation I had told her to "go find out what the world is, or isn't, doing about it." She took me literally (of course) and before we knew it, the A21 Campaign had birthed. In what can only be called a miracle story, it has become possibly the most holistic and effective human-trafficking response agency in the world. I could be biased, but the fruit of this ministry speaks for itself.

The agency is independent of Hillsong but is connected heart and soul and is our chosen partner in addressing this global problem. The campaign now has offices on a number of continents and takes up the challenge from four angles: awareness, prevention, rescue, and prosecution. Colour had the honor of playing a strategic role in raising initial awareness and stirring leaders, churches, and anyone who cared to be involved. As mentioned in previous chapters, we all have a local world to be mindful of, but there are some global issues that need collaborative strength for any outcome to be achieved. Human trafficking is a massive issue that cannot be addressed by merely one or two willing hearts—it's going to take a concerted effort by many, in the realm of both the natural and the spiritual, if results are to be seen.

So into this mix, our first-ever victim had been rescued. For reasons of safety we are not using her real name, but I will call her Lora.

She was Ukrainian and had been trafficked at eighteen years of age and held captive for four years. She had been miraculously rescued and was in our first shelter in Greece. Christine desperately wanted her to experience Colour and had organized for her to come home to Kiev. My first encounter with this sweet, pretty girl was in the hallway of the Palace Ukraine venue in Kiev, and I will never forget her first words: With broken English and a smile as wide as the ocean, she said to me, "I can smile again, I can smile again."

The depravity and atrocities these enslaved girls endure are beyond imagination. Lora had come from a place of captivity to a place of rescue and embrace, and had then flown with the team to Kiev. As the plane landed, she said a smile came upon her face because she realized that all the dreams she had ever had (and thought she had lost) seemed suddenly possible. She simply could not stop smiling.

In this fleeting hallway moment with a tiny Ukrainian girl, the lights went on again. Proverbs 31 says that "she smiles at the future." I've loved and taught these verses for years, yet I'd only seen them in one context. That day, Lora's words helped me see yet another layer within the whisper. The Spirit of God opened my eyes to the smile *within* the smile and the fact that the captive (the truly captive, enslaved, severely abused, and endlessly raped) was within this beautiful truth.

I'm pretty sure the entire host of heaven smiled that day, knowing that a company of daughters had proven to be their little sister's keeper. They had prayed for her when they didn't know her, they had facilitated her rescue, and they were now committed to her well-being.

The Life of One and the Power of One

There are so many stories—this next girl I'll call Viktoria, Vika for short. She was abducted in the rural villages of Ukraine, where she was forced to service countless men every day. One day, Vika was working the street when suddenly she stood on a hidden land mine. It exploded and blew shrapnel through her legs. Her traffickers saw this happen—they got in their truck and instead of rescuing her, instead of taking this poor child to a hospital, they ran over her. They callously and cruelly ran over her with the truck until they thought she was dead, and then they drove away. Unbelievable. Vika somehow survived and ended up in the care of our A21 friends in Ukraine. Caring partners raised the $35,000 needed for her surgery, and her legs were repaired. I remember Chris sending me pictures of X-rays from the hospital that I still have on my phone.

I met this young woman one Sunday in the big, white, igloo-looking building that had become home to our Kiev church. I had been in the first morning service and was racing to the airport to return home. The Colour marathon for that year was over and I was keen to see my family and go comatose on the plane with a mindless movie. As I went into the small greenroom area of our church, they told me that Viktoria was in church for the first time and asked if I would like to meet her. Of course I wanted to meet this brave young woman. They wheeled her in and, to be honest, emotion got the better of me.

I knelt down beside this beautiful young woman in the wheelchair and gently said, "Viktoria, I am so honored to meet you." Choking back the tears, I undid a tiny diamond-cross necklace that a friend had given me in London the week prior and gently placed it around her delicate neck. With someone interpreting, I told her she was beautiful. My friend Laura (who played Mary Poppins in London's West End for many years) was also in the room with a Bible in her hand. She had purchased it not knowing whom she would give it to, but she crossed the room and gifted it to this precious young woman.

I left for the airport exhausted and gloriously spent, as I always am at the end of these conferences. I later heard that Viktoria attended the next service. Dr. Robi Sonderegger, who had been my guest speaker that year, was speaking. Unbeknownst to Robi, this young girl was in the service, and he had no idea of her story or circumstances. He spoke a message about forgiveness. He is a clinical psychologist with profound insight into the human condition, but more than that he understands the power of Christ-centered forgiveness. For many years he had worked in northern Uganda, helping traumatized victims overcome their savage experiences, showing them how to effectively forgive their oppressors. That morning, he shared these principles and the stories of a far-away land where people had suffered in a similar way to Viktoria. Could she have been in a more perfect service? That morning, she opened her heart to the King of heaven. She accepted Him as Lord and Savior and chose the process of forgiveness toward those who had done all manner of evil against her.

The following year I was back again in Kiev and I asked after Viktoria. They pointed to a beautiful, tall, dark-haired girl sitting along the same row. I couldn't believe my eyes. I hadn't recognized her as I walked past, and yet here she was—as pretty as a picture, radiant, no evident scars, worshipping and entering into the goodness of God and life. She had recovered and was (if memory serves me correctly) working as a fitness instructor. Only the grace of God can do this—the relentless love of God and the embrace of people who understand and are prepared to do all for the sake of the one. How perfect is our Savior—He came into an insane, brutal, and violent world with the intent to restore life, and life in abundance (see John 10:10).

Twenty-seven million is an overwhelming statistic until you meet the one. When that happens, it doesn't matter how much it costs, it doesn't matter how much effort is needed—the one matters!

The smile to die for in both these young women (and all the other rescued girls we have met) was worth dying for. It was worth the effort, the labor, the long hours, the prayer offered, and the tears shed. Their freedom was on our watch and by the grace of God, we were not going to disappoint them—or the many others still waiting for us in the future.

• twenty •

CUPCAKES, FREEDOM FIGHTERS, AND WEAPONS OF WAR

(The Sounds of Freedom)

Freedom has many faces.

I'm not sure what freedom means to you. On the marginally safer end of the spectrum, freedom might be defined as "unrestricted ease of movement." Share this definition with someone who has lost mobility and they'll more than likely nod in reminiscent agreement. Their entire world may have been altered by injury or disease. I have a family member suffering from a debilitating disease, and the loss of movement is creating endless frustrations that she has no option but to overcome.

Midspectrum, the word can be defined as "the power to speak, act, and think as one desires." A romantic ideal, fabulously true while thinking is correct and society is on the straight and narrow. All who advocate freedom will approach this definition from their own bias, yet life is not measured by ideal alone. Life is measured and judged by the outcome. Jesus unapologetically said, "You will recognize them by their fruits" (Matt. 7:16 ESV). In some parts of the world, so-called freedom of thought, speech, and action among extreme and misguided people groups has brought nothing but sorrow to bear on society—our current terrorist wars are testimony to that. Human life is either precious or not. I'm glad I stand on the side that regards all life as precious, that advocates words of life, not death, and that continually challenges the renewal of thinking to that which is true, honorable, just, pure, lovely, and commendable (see Phil. 4:8 ESV).

And then, of course, the face of freedom to the slave means the absence of domination and bondage. Despotism and tyranny are definitely on the extreme end of the spectrum, with lack of freedom (enslavement) having within its meaning "servitude, hard labor, oppression, toil, grind," and plain old unhappiness.

So the fight for freedom in all its diversity is complex, to say the least. It has many faces, it involves all manner of cause and effect, and it requires response from many angles. Yet, if all was pared back to what is truly foundational, we might find that the complexities that ail the human heart (where freedom or lack thereof begins) are not dissimilar. The role of the church (and the Sisterhood within it) is to point people to truth and create pathways that lead people toward purpose, fulfillment, happiness, and ultimately freedom.

All these will never become reality unless the fundamental diseases within the human heart are addressed. The planet needs more than a giant Band-Aid—it needs to be healed from the inside out.

Pathways Home

I have three beautiful daughters, and their individual pathways to ease, happiness, and freedom have all been different. Two of these daughters we gloriously inherited when my sons chose their wives, and one I had the honor and blessing to birth and raise. They're all around the same age—beautiful young women with much to offer life.

When Laura was born, the boys were seven and five. A part of me could have easily stopped with them—life was full, and I didn't quite know how to add a third baby to the mix. My reasoning: I have two hands, two boys, and if we add another, I need to grow a third arm to cope. Are any of you nodding in agreement? Brian is a brilliant father, but we were madly planting a young church, we didn't have the finances to hire additional help, and I was pretty much a full-time working mom juggling a million of those proverbial plates. But something within wasn't content to stop with two little boys—we wanted a third child, and of course my deep desire was for a little girl. I read Psalm 37:4 again and madly delighted myself in the Lord, hoping that the desire of my heart was His also.

So into our world she landed on February 26, 1987, nine pounds twelve ounces and twenty-three and a half inches long. Her older brother Joel beat her by a few ounces and half an inch, although he has grown into a skyscraper and she is just perfect—hashtag fav! (Okay, that is an affectionate inside family joke. #allmyfavorites.)

Pastoring a church places you in the public eye, and there was much expectation for her to be a girl. Back in the mid-eighties (which sounds quite ancient now), scans were not the norm, so we had no idea what sex this baby was before she was born. I was seriously content to have another son, but the well-meaning pressure was getting to me toward the end, along with my gigantic belly and swollen ankles.

I birthed her in an inner-city Catholic hospital during Sydney's Gay and Lesbian Mardi Gras, which created no end of intrigue to observe from the nursery windows at two a.m. (night feed). I was immediately besotted with this bundle of pink with rosebud lips and perfect temperament. Even when she was a newborn, I would tuck her into her cot and kiss her little neck a million times till she gave me a little grin, closed her eyes, and fell asleep. Don't hate me if you had babies who were a little more challenging—trust me, we've had our moments also—but these are my first memories of my Laura Elizabeth.

When Brian went to church that Sunday, he walked into our warehouse facility and across the back of the stage in giant hand-cut pink letters he saw the words IT'S A GIRL! Everyone was so happy and ready to celebrate this child who had entered all our lives. Little did I know that those same words ("it's a girl") would frame the Sisterhood in years to come and provide a (now) hilarious memory of a Colour opener involving an artistically filmed birth-canal re-enactment that strangely resembled the waterslides at some fun water park...Oh, that's right, that birth-canal scene *was* the waterslide at Wet 'n Wild. Feel free to have a wee giggle.

My other daughters are equally lovely.

Lucille and Esther are both stunning young women who have captivating stories of growing up, finding their feet, and finding the paths that ultimately led them home. I won't lie and say that any of my three girls have had picture-perfect lives. They haven't, but then can that be said of any of us? It is so easy to observe others and mistakenly think that everything in their world is perfect without knowing or understanding the complexities of life they may have experienced.

Most of us may never suffer enslavement or the brutalities perpetrated against Viktoria or Lora, but unhappiness within the human soul can be as disturbing and dangerous. The kind of unhappiness that leads to despondency, which then leads to despair and worse, is as much a destroyer as any tyrannical oppressor—it just wears a different face. The pursuit of happiness looks different the world over; however, scratch the surface of the human heart anywhere and you find people searching for that elusive something that will prove there is more to life. It's the pursuit of *more* that often leads people down imperfect paths, the consequence being loss of freedom in one form or another.

Freedom and Belonging

So back to my kids: When Joel married Esther, they found themselves in Ibiza, playground of the rich and famous. For the record, they're neither rich nor famous, but it seems heaven may have a plan for them to salt the lives of people at this end of society. They'd fallen in love, and their wedding tale is another book in itself. They decided to get married with two weeks' notice for everyone—can I pause here to say God bless them (so happy) and God bless us (hello) for turning our entire world upside down to be in New York during one of the busiest seasons in our calendar. For reasons Esther can share if she one day decides to, she chose to invite only her parents, brother, and cousin from Brazil. In a whirlwind of craziness and fun, and with only fifty guests pressed into a boutique hotel in SoHo, they tied the knot on a wintry Tuesday evening. When she walked into the room in a pale yellow gown and white fur wrap, my big handsome son put his arm around me and said, "Mum...a whole nuther level, right?" He was besotted and bedazzled—in fact, I think we all were.

They delayed their honeymoon, heading to Europe when they could schedule time away. There Esther looked forward to introducing some of her old (and absent from the wedding) friends to her new husband. In this context, they found themselves sitting outside a club in the glamorous Spanish playground.

As she tells the story, my new daughter looked across the table at my son, who had gone a little quiet, and said, "Joel, are you okay?" He paused and then replied, "I don't feel like I belong." She looked back at him and said, "Joel...nobody feels like they belong...*nobody*."

Nobody feels like they belong. Pause and ponder that for a moment. In essence, what was being said was: It doesn't matter that everybody is draped in designer clothes and all the trimmings that go with this lifestyle; it doesn't matter that they all have super-model good looks; it doesn't matter if they all appear to be living some kind of dream and this world feels and acts exclusive. *Nobody feels like they belong.* Esther went on to tell me that, prior to finding Christ in her own experience, she honestly thought that everyone in the entire world felt alone. To her, everyone was on the same page regardless of whether they were a homeless person on the side-walk or someone with a calendar full of fabulous dinner dates who had people hanging off them day and night. She honestly believed that loneliness was the human condition.

Never-Ever Land

The elusive pursuit of freedom, with all its associated illusions and side effects, is the challenge facing society. There isn't a person alive who isn't chasing happiness or seeking fulfillment in some form or other. For many, it becomes an endless string of crossroads, where decisions made will either lead them perfectly or lead them astray. And without Jesus, it too often proves a difficult and bumpy ride toward an elusive never-ever land.

It's the challenge the Son of God came to address; it's the chal-lenge that the church has to bring uncondemning clarity to; and it's the challenge front and center of this Sisterhood. Fighting for the freedom of the furthest heart embraces the entire spectrum of encumbered society—from the literal captive within a dark and filthy brothel to the (captive) housewife who behind the perfect picket-fence facade hates her existence, to the (captive) schoolgirl being sold a lie about her personhood and value. The fight involves empathetic Christlike awareness, concern, and response for those caught in the quest for answers, fulfillment, or a better way.

Boot Camp

To this end, those within the true heart and spirit of Sisterhood have been gathered, equipped, and mobilized. To this end, the Spirit of God has compelled and rallied us like the troops mentioned in Micah. A new wineskin has taken shape, enabling everyday girls to step in and engage the battle with renewed precision. And to this lovely and glorious end, the women whom Jesus had been waiting for (remember the vision of Jesus waiting for the women) were becoming not just an ideal or idea, an event, or a conference—they were becoming a force for good and a movement that was being felt on the ground.

This fight for freedom didn't require literal recruitment or boot camp. It didn't require military training or a "tour of duty" season away from family and friends. It was instead an army of girls with a passion to step into the fray wherever it presented.

• *Recruitment was recruitment of the heart.* If you allowed yourself to hear the cry of the ailing or afflicted, regardless of whether the cry was in a faraway land or in the room next door, you were recruited.

• *Boot camp was the Word.* The unchanging Word of God was coming alive in our hearts and was training us to be exactly who Christ intended when He chose, appointed, and planted us (see John 15:16 AMP). Boot camp was our awakening to the "because factor" spoken of in Isaiah 61. The Word was teaching us that the Holy Spirit (who empowered Jesus) was the same Spirit who would enable, anoint, and empower our everyday hearts. He was teaching us how to bring healing to the brokenhearted, sight to the blind, freedom to the captive, and the gospel of good news to the poor.

And the lessons will always be ongoing, because the landscape of this world in dire need is continually changing and we therefore need the ongoing genius of God's Spirit.

• *Boot camp was in the roll call.* Turning up and staying at one's post was important. Each year, those who felt connected and commissioned would make their annual pilgrimage, and as the revelation grew in their hearts, they would eagerly preregister in the thousands to secure their seat and place in the future.

• *Boot camp was in the gathering and scattering.* The "I Am Sisterhood" declaration was being engraved into our core reality and was finding expression in churches all around the world. A new passion for one's church and planting was shaping a new breed of women within local churches, with local pastors and leaders alike noticing the fruit, recognizing the mantle, and encouraging their girls to attend.

Like the great host of women spoken of in Psalm 68, we would gather and then scatter (again and again and again) with the intent to carry and proclaim the hope-infused Word back to wherever home was. "The Lord gives the word [of power]; the women who bear and publish [the news] are a *great host*" (Ps. 68:11 AMP, emphasis mine).

The response strategies that so often dropped unexpectedly into my spirit in the dawn hours, or on a plane when sleep proved elusive, then grew in clarity and precision as those around the planning tables captured the vision and added their genius to what they were about. I came to recognize these as "the dawn strategies"— those unusual moments around three a.m. when you honestly wonder, "Did an angel just tap me awake and seed something from above?" Isaiah challenges us to be awake and alert. Sometimes I wonder if the dawn hours aren't part of God's perfect timing to speak, because body, soul, and spirit are rested and hopefully removed from the distractions that contend for our attention during the day.

> *Get out of bed*, Jerusalem! *Wake up*. Put your face in the sunlight. GOD's bright glory has risen for you. The whole earth is wrapped in darkness, all people sunk in deep darkness, But GOD rises on you, his sunrise glory breaks over you. Nations will come to your light, kings to your sunburst brightness. Look up! Look around! Watch as they gather, watch as they approach you: Your sons coming from great distances, your daughters carried by their nannies. When you see them coming you'll smile—big smiles! Your heart will swell and, yes, burst! All those people returning by sea for the reunion, *a rich harvest* of exiles gathered in from the nations! (Isaiah 60:1–5 MSG, emphasis mine)

A New Industry

And so to this end, the Colour gifts (the two-dollar mirrors, the rubber gloves, and the symbols of value) morphed into uncanny and unlikely weapons of warfare! Cupcakes and teapots, water bottles and T-shirts, knitting needles and prayer journals, money boxes and colorful paint cans (and not least, beautifully created Bibles to pass on to others) were added to the ongoing story and became the means that helped mobilize our Sisterhood-hearts and facilitate inroads into many of these pressing humanitarian needs.

If lawyers, tactical teams, and insane resources were needed to rescue an enslaved sister, then we would learn how to strategize to make that happen and support those called to be on the front line.

If stretching the monthly finances to help an impoverished

child or an HIV/AIDS–suffering woman was needed, then we would grow our capacity to include them in our family budget.

If discipline was needed to throw on a pair of sneakers in order to "walk and pray" for sisters, cities, and streets, then disciplined we would become. The sidewalks became our altar. Increased fitness may have been an added bonus, but spiritual muscles were being flexed and eternal fruit was being fought for in the heavens.

If any number of our diverse and widespread projects needed support, we would learn how to gather our equally diverse and wide-spread friends to network around a kitchen table or café counter in order to bring ease to their circumstance and strength to their failing hearts.

Our catch cry and war cry to *be the change* became the strategy around a new Colour industry designed to equip the girls with tools to facilitate change in the everyday settings of everyday life. Who could have imagined that the clink of a teacup, the click of some knitting needles, the sound of sneakers on the sidewalk, and the rattle of coins in a can could become the deafening sounds of freedom? But they did. China may have a Little Red Book in their history, but we invented another Little Red Book with five hundred ways to be the change in local community and society. With devoted precision, we labored to remove every fear or excuse and upskill the least likely (and the most likely) so that together we could make a difference.

As my own spirit and mind fine-tuned to what God was asking of us, I remember gathering our creative team and encouraging them that these gifts could no longer be trinkets that end up in the trash or are left behind in hotel rooms. The dynamics had changed—no longer were we ordering a few hundred gifts, we were ordering literally thousands of gifts and shipping them around the world, and I wasn't prepared to waste the investment. My conviction was that we either attach these gifts to the cause and make them work for the cause, or we don't do them! All were in agreement, and should the day come when we don't give a gift at Colour, I'm confident the girls attending will not judge me unfairly for this.

All Ends of Society

All ends of society need to hear the good news that they are not forgotten and that there is a God in heaven who believes in them. On a panel relating to human trafficking, I heard my daughter-in-law Esther comment that the girls at the top end of society sell their souls as easily as those on the other end—they're all equally entrapped in the pursuit of something "better" or "more." Therefore, the battle for freedom also requires an army of willing players on all ends of society.

There will be those on the front lines. They're the ones who feel the heat and touch the need right where it is, but those on the midlines or back lines are just as important. Never diminish or undervalue any of the players who make an army strong.

Those who raise awareness or enlarge their capacity to be financial supporters are critical because the highways and byways of lost and hurting humanity cost money. It costs nothing except compassion and time to engage a person in the gutter, but creating effective pathways out of the gutter for that person is another story. As the saying goes, the gospel message is free but it takes money to take it to those in need of hearing it.

The ones who stay at home and keep the fires burning with prayer and faithful commitment to church and planting are as essential as those who literally stare down the enemy on the front line. The battle is so often won by the girls in their living rooms, kitchens, or bedrooms—they're the ones who in prayer and supplication push back the darkness, creating a way for miracle breakthroughs.

Something's Missing

The Sisterhood is a menagerie of wild and wonderful girls. They come in every shape, size, and color. They're young and gorgeous and full of life—and they're old and gorgeous and full of life. They're the country gals and the city gals. Some wear fashion suits and designer heels, and some wear sweats and Birkenstocks. They're the everyday sweethearts who are heaven's delightful (and delighted-in) daughters, through whom His love affair with this lost and broken world is being played out.

Songwriter John Mayer has a song called "Something's Missing." He sings of the constant search for happiness and wholeness in the physical world, where it seems like we're never complete.

Suffice to say the world is searching for the elusive "something"—money, friends, popularity, sex, fame and fortune, peace and freedom, contentment and fulfillment—but the elusive something is not as elusive as some would think. It's simply that there is an enemy seeking to conceal it because when truth is concealed, freedom is compromised. The Bible clearly and unapologetically says that it is truth (and truth alone) that sets the human soul free—and truth, in all its fullness, is found in none other than Jesus Christ. "And ye shall know the truth, and the truth shall make you free" (John 8:32 KJV).

The fight for freedom begins with people like you and me discovering our own personal truth, which can then become a contagious lifeline for others.

My daughter-in-law Esther and her two inherited sisters, Laura and Lucille, each had to find their own "truth north" that led them to personal freedom. Their pathways were all different, as are yours and mine, as are the pathways of the multitudes still wandering without direction or understanding, or still standing at crossroads not knowing which direction to take.

Freedom has many faces and many candidates and will require many different and varied responses from all of us. Answers to the many complex questions and issues within this current world scene will come only as each of us finds our own personal freedom and we then play our small (or large) part in this giant puzzle called *life*.

Real freedom is also magnetic. My prayer is that you'll become an inspiring and magnetic force in your own world, and like the King's daughter in Psalm 45, that many will follow you into that same beautiful, expansive, and wide-open space called freedom.

twenty-one

AMBUSH IN THE AIR

(The Prayer Maps)

I guess the bad guys had no idea that they were outnumbered by a host of housewives with map in hand and a fierce determination to foil their plans and ambush the enemy at his own game.

Google the "history of maps" and it will tell you (among other things) that maps were invaluable tools for ancient rulers, traders, and military leaders—an interesting piece of info considering the tenor of this chapter. Google "prayer" and you'll find everything from meditation on mountain peaks to bended knee in cathedrals. Google "How many prayers have been answered?" or "How many sermons have ever been spoken on prayer?" and Mr. Google cuts a blank, because prayer is an eternal mystery and has been with us since the beginning of time.

It's also somewhat of a wonder.

It connects the human soul with the Creator; it changes the atmosphere in and around our lives; it soothes, strengthens, heals, and empowers; it unleashes the impossible and it makes a way for the miraculous—it also *wins the battle*.

Before Jesus returned to heaven, He kindly taught His followers how to pray: "After this manner therefore pray ye: Our Father which art in heaven, Hallowed be thy name. Thy kingdom come,

Thy will be done in earth, as it is in heaven" (Matt. 6:9–10 KJV). The book of James exhorts us to pray for one another, and encourages us that the fervent and effectual prayer of right-standing people accomplishes much. We are also instructed in the book of Ephesians that after dressing in the full armor of God, we should stand and *pray*. In fact, the entire Bible is full of those who persevered and won the diverse battles of their day because they prayed.

The Global Table

I believe that the weapon the Church of Jesus Christ must bring to this current global table of unrest and crisis is prayer. It's a weapon that many outside of faith may never truly understand or appreciate—but regardless of whether they do or don't, prayer is what engages the spiritual realm, which is so often the core and cause of today's problems.

The human heart makes its own choices and can often get itself into all sorts of self-inflicted trouble, but this doesn't negate a spiritual realm that does exist—a realm that is a constant battlefield between what is right and wrong, good and evil, Christlike and anti-Christ.

Displace the spiritual darkness, and what is just and correct has an opportunity to penetrate and filter into the situation. Displace the spiritual darkness, and the bad guys will retreat elsewhere, because the Bible says that those who perpetrate evil love darkness more than light. Like nasty insects or cockroaches, they'll race for darkened cover when the light is turned on. Throw a spotlight on the shadowlands where horrid practices thrive, and results will be seen. Displace spiritual-enemy darkness, and there is margin for intervention.

It was in this context that we invented a new strategy for the Sisterhood.

If there is one thing women are renowned for, it's *prayer*. I think I've always known this, and I had always wanted to create some form of prayer network within the Sisterhood, but if I'm also honest, the idea was easier than the reality (and logistics) of doing so, especially on a national level, with many women coming from other denominations and fellowships. I may also have been marginally scarred by my own failure in a 24-hour prayer chain.

Way back in the early days, my church in New Zealand called a very important prayer chain. I can't remember what the issue was (oops) but I volunteered for the midnight hour. How romantic. I got myself all settled in my mother's living room—blanket, pillow, Bible, and heater (it was a cold night in Kiwiland). I patiently waited for midnight to arrive, when my important and critical contribution to the well-being of the planet would be made. I waited, waited, waited...and then suddenly it was two a.m. What?! No! I had completely fallen asleep, completely stuffed up, and *completely failed the chain!* Dear God, the midnight link had been left wide open. If all hell broke out over my beloved nation, it was my doing! I had tragically fallen asleep on my volunteered watch, and if the world came to an end that night, it was *my fault.* Hilarious as I now recall this.

Thank God those days of naive intensity have passed. For all I know, Jesus probably smiled and thought, "Oh, look, she's fallen asleep...bless...love the intent, love the heater, love the blankie, adorable...maybe I'll cover this one." After all, the Bible does say that Jesus hasn't stopped interceding for us, even when we accidentally goof off (see Rom. 8:34 and Ps. 121:3–4).

The truth is, the world isn't going to come to an end because you missed your cue. However, the world may well come to an end if we *all* keep missing our cues and if we never fully understand the power of the heaven partnership we are in. Prayer is a critical element that fuels the plan and the miracle-working power of God. It helps the will of God penetrate this earthly realm and bring much-needed answers. *Thy kingdom come, Thy will be done on earth as it is in heaven* is the most power-packed prayer we can ever utter. And prayer is indeed a mystery. One day we will surely understand from an eternal perspective, but in the meantime, let's simply be obedient to what the Word commands us to do.

Don't Stop Yet

I have so many stories where prayer made the difference, and I'm sure you do also. Like the time a little boy in our world nearly drowned: By the time his family got him to the hospital, the prognosis was grim; doctors said, "If he survives the night it will be a miracle, but he will surely have severe brain damage."

Our church rallied to prayer. That afternoon, his mother, Robyn, went into the bathroom because the situation was not improving—her mother-heart was failing her, but she felt a whisper, almost a gentle rebuke within her that encouraged her not to give up and said, "*Pray in faith.*" As she walked back into the intensive care unit where her little son lay, she literally felt the presence of God enter the room. She later said it was as though she heard the rush of angel wings to his bedside.

A few hours later, her toddler opened his eyes, recognized his Thomas the Tank Engine, and asked for his breakfast. That little guy is Tyler Douglass—he's grown, he's perfect, and he's currently one of our fabulous Young & Free worship leaders and the brother of JD, whom many of you may know from Hillsong United. Perhaps when God whispered in Robyn's ears, He knew that His ministering angels were close with the miracle needed—perhaps they had just landed on the hospital roof or were on their way through the corridors, asking each other, "What room is he in again?"

Prayer works for all of us—we simply need to grow in the

revelation, understanding, and trust of it. I named this chapter "Ambush in the Air" because prayer also works en masse when we harness our strength and focus our efforts.

The Maps

So, in the perfect timing of God, the "Sisterhood Prayer Maps" came into play.

We weren't content to know that there were nations where young women by the thousands were being easily trafficked, and we weren't content to know that many of the borders and ports in these nations were porous, enabling the bad guys to have their evil way. Something had to be done! In all honesty, the majority of us couldn't suddenly become Rambo's sister and rush off to the front lines. We couldn't all romance the idea of working for the United Nations or the anti-trafficking agencies that were emerging—the vast majority of us had everyday lives to live, families to care for, responsibilities to be true to at home, yet what we could do is *pray*.

The Bible is full of stories about God ambushing the enemy through supernatural prayer. Why couldn't we also ambush the spiritual forces behind this insane and evil situation with supernatural prayer? Why couldn't we unleash a Psalm 68:11 host of prayer warriors with the intent of displacing the evil forces at work within men's hearts in order that rescue, solution, and change could happen? The Bible speaks of such heavenly warfare, and Psalm 10 speaks of "the wicked man" waiting in ambush to attack and devour the innocent—our intent was to ambush his ambush through prayer.

Our strategy would take the form of *fervent, effectual, authoritative prayer*.

Our strategy was to map the world and mark as many borders

and ports where trafficking happens as we could. A team began researching the "source and receiver nations"—in other words, the nations that facilitate the biggest supply of trafficked girls and the nations that have the biggest demand for these girls. We began researching the fundamental deficits and complexities within many of these nations in an effort to give our girls (our prayer warriors) tangible things to pray about.

We could and would definitely "pray in the Spirit" (Eph. 6:18), but we would also pray with intelligent understanding. The Proverbs 31 woman is described as an intelligent and virtuous woman. "Virtuous" isn't something old-fashioned and passive; it has within its meaning "a force"—a force we were determined to become.

It wasn't only a case of praying "Father, please help the victims" (which, by the way, works)—it included prayers that were aimed at the source of the problems. If unemployment was an issue, let's pray about unemployment. If corruption in government was a root issue, then let's pray intelligently about that. If we were dealing with deep-rooted issues that diminish the value of womanhood and make women easy fodder, then let's begin praying fervently that miraculous change would begin in the decision-makers and culture-masters of these places.

Audacious

Perhaps our vision was audacious. Could criminal cartels and mafia lords be foiled by prayer? Could long-standing cultures be challenged and laws changed, and could lives really be rescued by the prayer of a bunch of unassuming women from all walks of life and corners of the earth? Eternity will one day bear witness, but we honestly felt that this was a God-given strategy—so we chose to obey, offer the strategy to the women, and leave the rest with God.

With the help of a remarkable team, I launched this prayer strategy at Colour 2010, with around four thousand Prayer Maps snapped up from the Sisterhood table.

Our desire to pay attention to the needs of "orphans, sisters, and nations" suddenly jumped to yet another level. Later that year, we heightened the focus with our own Hillsong girls in our campuses around the world, encouraging every woman in our church (potentially many thousands) to choose at least one nation on the map and make that nation her own.

I can't say how many picked up the challenge and bought into the initiative, but those who did were encouraged to stick their map on the fridge, tuck it within their Bible, or hang it off a file cabinet at work—and whenever it was seen, may it serve as a reminder to pray for girls who might be in the process of seduction and abduction. May these maps hauntingly remind us that a girl right now might be in a shipping container or in the back of a van, being taken across a border; or perhaps an evil plan is being hatched in that very moment, a plan that needs spiritual intervention to sabotage it and bring it to naught.

Only heaven will truly measure what happens when we pray, but remarkably our A21 (human-trafficking agency) friends witnessed unprecedented breakthroughs in the immediate season following the launch of this initiative.

Certain nations where traffickers had never been prosecuted were suddenly seeing traffickers arrested, tried, fined, and jailed. My friend Christine will tell you that whenever we pumped the Prayer Maps, girls would be rescued within a day or two. On one occasion during the Kiev conference, we were fervently praying about this issue when suddenly the phone of one of our workers rang. She was on the front or second row. It was the police, calling to advise that *yet another girl* had just been rescued and was coming to the shelter that afternoon.

God Bless Instagram

One day, I felt compelled to Instagram and tweet the Colour Sisterhood from my home in Sydney and encourage them to pray specifically for the "-stan" nations of eastern Europe. I texted our team in Ukraine, asking them to confirm these exact nations—and maybe spell them for me (hello).

Kazakhstan, Uzbekistan, Kyrgyzstan, Tajikistan, Turkmenistan. I posted the prayer request, including with it what we call "the RU," or "Russian-speaking nations"—Russia, Ukraine, Belarus, Moldova, Azerbaijan, Georgia, Armenia, Estonia, Latvia, and Lithuania.

Within literally a day or two, we heard that two girls had been miraculously rescued from Kazakhstan. Apparently they were not Christians, but one of them had looked heavenward and in desperation had prayed, "God, if you are real, please, please rescue us." And He did. God always hears the lament. Yet, as I wrote several chapters earlier, he also needs the prayer partnership of us on the ground. The battle needs prayer that will push back the darkness, confuse the enemy, and foil the plan. The battle needs prayer that declares the promise and goodness of God over the situation. The battle needs prayer that creates margin and opportunity where those who can step into the fray are ready and poised to move.

Two young lives across that vast expanse of European landmass may not seem like much to a skeptic, but to those two young girls and their families it was the miracle-working power of God. Who but God alone truly knows what else might have taken place amid that social-media-inspired prayer? Maybe we should take a moment, here and now, and offer up a prayer or two for the lives of those in desperate need:

Father, with You nothing is impossible.
In Your Name, dear Lord, we pray that You will
intervene and rescue. We take the prayer and
declaration of King David in Psalm 10 and we pray
it over the nations and continents of this earth,
over borders and ports and villages and towns . . .

The wicked in pride and arrogance hotly pursue and persecute the poor; let them be taken in the schemes which they have devised...

He thinks in his heart, I shall not be moved...

He sits in *ambush* in the villages; in hiding places he slays the innocent...

[The prey] is crushed, sinks down; and the helpless falls by his mighty [claws]. [The foe] thinks in his heart, God has quite forgotten; He has hidden His face; He will never see [my deed].

Arise, O Lord! O God, lift up Your hand; forget not the humble [patient and crushed]...

O Lord, *you have heard* the desire and the longing of the humble and oppressed; You will *prepare and strengthen and direct their hearts*, You will cause Your ear to hear,

To do justice to the fatherless and the oppressed, *so that man, who is of the earth, may not terrify them any more.* (Psalm 10 AMP, emphasis mine)

Amen.

If you have had anything to do with rescued girls, you'll know that God can strengthen them in their captivity. We have stories of girls who suddenly saw an opportunity for escape and somehow, amid paralyzing fear and intimidation, found the inner strength to take that opportunity and run. He indeed can "prepare and strengthen and direct" them. Don't underestimate the power of prayer—who knows if it was your prayer, or that of a girlfriend, that fueled their courage?

A House of Prayer

The gospels record Jesus walking into the temple and, in a display of passion, zeal, and anger, declaring what Isaiah prophesied: "My house will be called a house of prayer for all nations" (Isa. 56:7).

Governments, law enforcement agencies, and the like all have a job to do in fighting the crimes of which I am writing, crimes that for the most part are perpetrated against Earth's precious daughters. Where corruption doesn't interfere, they do the best they can, but as I said previously, what we as faith-filled believers within His church bring to the table is what they often don't have. God's house in these latter days has to be a house of offered and answered *prayer*. As the church, we don't need fanfare, we don't need to be acknowledged or thanked. What we need to do is enter our closet, close the door, and pray as the Spirit of God directs.

The Maggies of This World

What we need to do is be inspired by the Maggies of this world. Maggie and her friends come from Surrey, England. Maggie is in her mid-to-late seventies. When she first heard about the maps and the plight of trafficked girls, she decided that this was something she and her friends could do. They could pray. They regularly meet in Maggie's living room. After tea, coffee, and cake (she's very English and very adorable), they pull out the maps. They then sit, each holding a map, and without trumpets, fuss, or drama they quietly pray over the borders, lives, and situations within these nations.

Well, the awesome praise report relating to Maggie and her little prayer warriors is that while they were gently and yet authoritatively praying for these nations, a trafficking ring in their own village was mysteriously foiled. There was a brothel literally under their noses that was dealing in trafficked girls. Don't tell me prayer doesn't work! Who knows what was happening in the other nations they were praying for, but the residue of their prayers affected their own local neighborhood. We filmed Maggie and her friends and showed their story at Colour one year. The women cheered, smiling from ear to ear, and it has possibly become one of our all-time favorite map stories.

Yes, who could imagine that some dear and delightfully English and proper little ladies could influence events and bring the bad guys down? I think we should all be encouraged to have another go. Maybe you've lost your map or never had one. Go online (www .coloursisterhood.com) and download a nation or need that resonates with your heart. I have no intention of these being unavailable, because precious lives hang in the balance of our prayer life.

One More Story

I love this story and will leave it with you as I begin to bring this chapter to a close. The fight for justice always starts with awareness. As you will have gathered, the issue of trafficking is front and center of the Sisterhood story. World authorities say that human trafficking is the second-largest criminal industry after drug dealing. It is as large an industry as the supply of illegal weapons and arms, and it is not going away. Sadly, I'm not sure it will ever be fully dealt with, and unprecedented migrant exodus from troubled nations is feeding the problem even more. However, the magnitude of these issues shouldn't stop us fighting for the ones who can be rescued. Awareness, prevention, education, rescue, and prosecution are the strategy. In this story, awareness proved the catalyst of rescue.

Our worship team from Kiev had been invited to an event in Slovakia. Their plane was delayed, and as the team sat killing time in the airport, some of the young men in the team noticed a handful of girls with a strange woman. They had eagerly served at Colour and had therefore listened to the Sisterhood sessions—*and were now aware that trafficking happens in their own backyard*. As they sat observing the girls, it became apparent that something was not right with these young women. In their words, the six young women were poorly dressed and appeared scared and sad. In contrast, the woman with them was well dressed and constantly on her phone as she corralled them.

The well-dressed woman momentarily left the area, and our team went into action. Trying not to frighten anyone, they quickly approached the girls, seeking to ask if they were okay. They were not okay! Only one could speak Russian and they were all from Moldova. They had no money, documents, or phones and had had no food for two days. Eventually, one girl opened up and said they were headed to Syria and had been promised jobs there, but only after they had signed strange documents that they were now fearful about. Two of them had young children back in the village and they were afraid for their safety.

The controlling woman strangely vanished from the airport (she had obviously observed the intervention), and it became very apparent that these girls were being trafficked into a horrific situation.

Thankfully, awareness on the part of our team allowed these poor girls to be noticed, and perhaps prayer on the part of someone in another part of the world allowed a plane to be delayed and a trafficker to be momentarily removed, which then allowed for a collision of lives that resulted in the rescue of six young women from a terrible fate. As soon as the police and official trafficking authorities arrived, the departure board lit up, announcing that our team's plane was no longer delayed. The Moldovan girls went on to be helped and restored to their families. Dear reader, feel free to smile, say a hearty amen, or do a little victory dance around your chair—because prayer and awareness ambushed the ambush!

An Indispensable Weapon

In the latter part of Paul's letter to the Ephesians he says, "*God's Word* is an indispensable weapon. *In the same way, prayer* is essential in this ongoing warfare. Pray hard and long. Pray for your brothers and sisters. Keep your eyes open. Keep each other's spirits up so that no one falls behind or drops out" (Eph. 6:15–18 MSG, emphasis mine). God is not willing that any fall behind, drop out, or get lost. Prayer is a critical weapon in this ongoing warfare.

I hope your heart is encouraged.

Prayer does work and God has you also in His sights. On a personal level, you may be going through a challenging season or you may feel like your situation is impossible. I want to encourage you that there may well be someone praying for you—someone you may never meet this side of eternity but someone who is being attentive to the leading and prompting of God's Spirit to pray. Don't despair and don't lose heart, and certainly don't stop hoping or praying yourself. Remember my friend Robyn in the hospital? She felt a whisper that prompted her not to give up but to keep praying until the answer arrived. If it helps, I personally just prayed for you as I wrote these words.

Our human tendency is to give up. When we are weakened we need others to pray and intercede for us. God's Spirit is well aware of those who need prayer and those who can pray—from heaven above, He is well able to coordinate the two and cause a fabulous collision of worlds and miracles.

David in Psalm 10 declares that God will prepare, strengthen, and direct the hearts of the oppressed until rescue comes. Allow Him to do that for you. Allow Him to be your source of strength, if that's what you need. Can I also encourage all of us to be that for others? When God awakens you in the night, instead of being agitated because you can't sleep, ask God if there is something or someone you should be praying for.

When you feel the nudge, please respond, because in all truthfulness it could be an urgent matter of life or death for the one on the other end of the equation.

twenty-two

GO HOME AND FLOURISH

(The Garden)

I f I were to be judged by the hashtag police, I'd probably be found guilty of chronic and annoying misuse.

The experts have much to say about social media etiquette, rules, and addictions. I'm actually aware and mindful of the dangers and traps, especially for young and vulnerable hearts. However, social media is also a fabulous tool that can be used for good.

For me personally, it creates an avenue to love on our church that these days numbers in the thousands, who are scattered far and wide around the globe. I find it remarkable that I can post something encouraging (or affectionate) to our "little Hillsong family" and within seconds have connection with whoever is up and interested. It allows for words of life to be exchanged; it allows for little glimpses into personal family life (which helps people know that you also are living in the real world), and it creates a platform to drive home kingdom truths that are actually important.

Scale of Eternity

If we could measure life on the scale of eternity, what's important to you? If you were to narrow down the key driving thoughts or words that frame your existence, passion, and purpose, what would they be? If you asked me that same question, I could possibly condense it to a handful of phrases that often salt my hashtag obsession.

• *#fav* weaves itself into anything that relates to the offspring. I may have snuck it in already in a previous chapter, but what's life if you can't have some fun with your kids? They all want to know if they're mom's favorite, and of course they all are, right?! Joel Timothy, you are my #fav firstborn. Ben, you are my #fav middle child, and Laura-belle, you are my #fav princess. Please don't think me trite—the world is a dark and sad place (and I have certainly been writing about that), but there is still plenty of room for love, affection, and playful banter.

• *#ilovemychurch* rates pretty high because I seriously love my church. I love everything about it. I love the vision, the adventure, and the people. I love the can-do volunteer spirit and the selfless spirit of servanthood that strengthens with each generation. I love the song in our house—not merely musical albums that chart in the industry, but rather songs that reflect the health, well-being, and devotion of passionate Christ followers. I love the spontaneity, fun, and lunacy, and I love the heart and soul of our church. These latter words have been used by many churches around the world, but they're more than clever or cute language—they're words that reflect the inner soul of a church (consisting of oceans of people from every walk of life) that exists to love and champion what is close to God's own heart.

• *#comeasyouare*, *#youbelonghere*, and *#thykingdomcome* are all perfect because they reflect salvation's bid. I don't know what your church culture is like, but in ours you can "come as you are"—exactly as you are, in fact, because that is exactly how Jesus loves us. We are living in a day of grace, and the prevailing words over the gospel invitation of the church to the world should be "Come as you are—you are welcome here!" Having said that, grace will never leave us as we are, but will always begin a work of transforming us into His likeness.

"You belong here" are words definitely within the fabric of faith's DNA. There are no exclusion clauses in heaven's invitation, and all people need to know they belong. A person's color, creed, culture, background, persuasion, sin, or past failings should not exclude them from discovering their personal worth and true personhood in Christ. Sadly, not all professing Christians think like this. I'm not talking about compromising what is scriptural and pure (because the last page in the Bible does say that what is unholy will not enter into heaven), but till that notable day the tenor of Scripture is full of saving grace toward the sinner. Our mandate is to cross every divide with the same compassion as Christ, and then graciously point people to the One who is well able to reveal all. Redemption is ongoing, so let's allow God to do the redeeming while we do the loving. Worthy of note is that while on Earth, Jesus judged only those who displayed an ugly and religious Pharisaic spirit toward others.

What is most important in any harvest field is that people see love *in action* so they experience firsthand that Jesus really is "the way and the truth and the life" (John 14:6).

And of course, "Thy kingdom come" hopefully needs no explanation. I save this little hashtag for the really big thoughts, the ones that involve us all and hopefully have our hearts welling with the knowledge that one day our "soon and coming King" will come.

• However...#*welcomehome* would have to be my all-time favorite. Many years ago, when we were building our first major facility, I labored to have WELCOME HOME etched into some glass at the front entrance. I had written a book called *Heaven Is in This House,* and the idea of church culture with a wide-open and all-embracive welcome mat was so important to me. I desperately wanted people to know that they were welcome and that, when they entered through the doors of what wasn't only Hillsong Church but the House of God, they were indeed *home.*

To the soul void of real love and family, these are not mere idle words—they're lifeblood! They're words that can introduce people to truth that will in turn nourish their lives and ultimately give them safe passage home, to where they need to be.

Flourish, Baby, Flourish

Home is where we are supposed to flourish, and home is where God does His finest work. Now, the reality of life is that not every natural or spiritual household is fabulous and lovely or conducive to growth and fruitfulness. Not every home is the garden God would have it be, and herein is another important challenge within this Sisterhood story.

For those reading who are pastors and leaders, we have a very sobering responsibility to make local church an environment of life—a garden wherein God can facilitate His heart toward individuals and families, a garden that will nurture men, women, children, and youth alike in a manner that causes people to flourish in everything they put their hand to. I've already mentioned Isaiah 61, but here it is again in the Message paraphrase: "For as the earth bursts with spring wildflowers, and as a *garden* cascades with blossoms, So the Master, GOD, brings righteousness into *full bloom* and puts praise on display before the nations" (Isa. 61:11 MSG, emphasis mine).

God's desire is that our lives flourish in such a stunning manner that they become a display of His goodness before all the nations.

The Poppies

With all these beautiful truths resonating, and ever-mindful that the God-whisper was about creating such an environment, we found ourselves gathered once again under one roof, with heaven watering and tending our lives. It was 2011 and the Colour Sisterhood had moved downtown and into the city. The prevailing language this year was "One Love, One Heart, One Sisterhood," and we were in the Sydney Entertainment Centre, a venue that hosted us for many years until it was demolished in order to be rebuilt. It had been a great conference and we felt like yet another wave of troops had been mobilized.

That year, our beloved friend Lisa Bevere was among our guest speakers. Lisa is actually way more than a guest—she really is family, and I feel that our hearts have been divinely knit. Our worlds collided in Manila, where she says she wept all night after hearing me speak about the Daughter of a King, because for years she felt she was writing prophetically of something she hadn't fully witnessed yet. When our lives did merge, and when she came and saw firsthand this Sisterhood in motion, she became one of the fabulous girlfriends with whom we intend to do life.

From where I sat in the venue, I had a great view of the stage. I'm usually a few rows up on the left-hand side, high enough to appreciate the sight of all the women and yet close enough to easily run the conference. It was the last night, and as always we try to seal the weekend with something special. I knew what was planned.

The stage was white, possibly our first-ever white stage. It was circular and huge because the venue is huge. Screens and images of softly cascading flowers were suspended above so that women in the far corners of the venue could see. We weren't officially in the round, but in some ways that's just what we were. When Lisa was finished speaking, the plan was that I would go back onstage and round off the conference with all that goes with ending such an event. It's always a little sad, because the girlfriends never want to say good-bye. We would then end with the exciting creative presentation we had prepared, which included the giant red poppies that were sitting perfectly around the edges of the stage, rising high into the air like big beautiful flowers growing up from a garden. I couldn't wait for this ending to happen and for the "kiss of heaven" to be upon that year's gathering.

So here I am amid all the beautiful imagery, listening to all Lisa was saying and mindful of what was to come, when all of a sudden the disturbing reality of the world we live in hit yet again. Lisa included a statistic in her sermon, and it appeared on the screens: 50 MILLION GIRLS MISSING ON THE EARTH TODAY BECAUSE OF GENDERCIDE. From where I sat, it was a harrowing visual contrast of life-and-death realities—beautiful images of flowers painting a picture of life as it should be, sandwiching a shocking statistic about Earth's daughters.

As the final moments in that year's conference drew to a close, I felt God speak to me yet again. In some ways it strangely felt like a second God-whisper, if that is remotely possible. In essence I felt our lovely Lord prompt me to get up after Lisa was finished and commission the girls as they left to return home. I sensed these words in my spirit:

When you get up at the very end to pray and farewell the girls,
    I want you to tell them something.
    I want you to tell them to *go home and flourish.*
    They want to make a difference; they want to change the world;
    and if they go home and flourish, they will.
    Tell them to flourish in their hearts; tell them to flourish in My Word;

tell them to flourish in their marriages, their parenting,
their neighborhood—
in whatever they do.
Tell them to *go home and flourish in their planting,*
in the place where I have planted them,
and if they do, they'll change the world.

The Gardens of Our Lives

So that's what I did. As the team sang about God being well able to
make beautiful things out of the dust of our lives, as giant red poppies slowly began to move and then rise from what now seemed like
the garden of that big old white stage, and as I shared these words,
an army of girls hopefully accepted the challenge to go home and
flourish.

It didn't matter if the garden of their lives was imperfect or in
disrepair. The challenge was to go home and try to make it better. If marriages were suffering, then let's be courageous enough to
make the adjustments needed. If kids or family (or any other relationship) were in need of attention, then let's go home and figure
how to refresh that relationship.

The raw reality, dear friends, is that if the example of our life
brings hope and testimony to that of another, enabling them to
change, then what we have essentially done is change the world.

Being a world changer is insanely possible for all of us, because if
enough of us were to flourish and excel in our parenting, then raising the next generation of world-class citizens and dynamic leaders would indeed change the world. If enough local churches were
to flourish, excel, and become the lighthouses they're called to be,
then local community and society would be positively influenced.
If enough of us were to flourish and excel in our careers, callings,

and God-entrusted gifts, then imagine what genius, invention, and solution would be added to the table. If enough of us were to flourish and excel in compassion and kindness, then the world would be less wounded and broken. And if enough of us were to flourish and excel in the life-changing Word of God, then imagine the wonder that would be unleashed upon the earth.

Indeed, if we were all to grow and flourish, the world would certainly be a better place. How wonderful that God would seal that 2011 gathering and kiss our lives with such a truth-worthy commission.

So that is how heaven landed our gathering that year, and that is how one of our all-time favorite hashtags came into being. #flourishBABYflourish became our catch cry and mantra for the months and journey ahead, and we had no end of positive fun with it... #loveBABYlove #believeBABYbelieve #dreamBABYdream #stretchBABYstretch #birthBABYbirth #prayBABYpray #breatheBABYbreathe #smileBABYsmile #danceBABYdance #shopBABYshop #funBABYfun are but a few that come to mind.

The Soil

If you have a conviction about where you are planted in life, then you truly need to know that the "soil" within that planting is well able to deliver what God has intended and ordained for your life. No soil is perfect. Like everything in life, soil needs to be cared for—it needs to be nourished, worked, watered, and rested. And when it is, the seeds of greatness within all our lives will have a place to take root and eventually emerge.

I'm not a fan of a mind-set that easily "church hops." We can and should be inspired by others, and sometimes visiting or having a season in a different place can certainly be part of the plan but, big picture, we weren't created to be wandering pot plants, regularly uprooting ourselves and having a little stint in every house or church along the street. We were created to be *the living planting of the Lord*, securely and perfectly sown, growing tall like the majestic cedars of Lebanon, positively contributing wherever God has planted us. My prayer is that you'll find your lifetime planting and that the wisdom of Psalm 92 will shape your world, enabling every good and perfect plan God has for you to be fulfilled:

> The [uncompromisingly] righteous shall flourish like the palm tree [be long-lived, stately, upright, useful, and fruitful]; they shall grow like a cedar in Lebanon [majestic, stable, durable, and incorruptible]. *Planted* in the house of the Lord, they shall flourish in the courts of our God. [*Growing in grace*] they shall still bring forth fruit in old age; they shall be full of sap [of spiritual vitality] and [rich in the] verdure [of trust, love, and contentment]. [They are living memorials] to show that the Lord is upright and faithful to His promises; He is my Rock, and there is no unrighteousness in Him. (Psalm 92:12–15 AMP, emphasis mine)

In the Great War of 1914–18, red field poppies emerged from the torn, devastated, and battle-scarred landscape of Belgium. In my nation (and others), these poppies have become the symbol of remembrance of those who fought and died in this and other wars. I don't know if our creative team who made these giant poppies by hand had these remembrance flowers in mind when we crafted this closing moment, but somehow the poppies added to the wonder of what was happening. In the eternal scheme of things, God is well able to cause beautiful things to emerge from the most broken and scarred places. I love the idea that we can flourish and salt the earth with similar color and life.

As an aside, I'd like to tell you that the big red Colour poppies are still alive and well, but alas they aren't. They were actually inverted beach umbrellas over which a devoted team sewed fabric and then attached green industrial hose as the stems. They gradually and tragically wilted as we lugged them around the world in our baggage from Sydney to Cape Town to London and then to Kiev—hilarious, because sometimes I feel exactly the same as I gloriously limp back to Sydney after a miraculous Colour marathon.

For those who love details, in Sydney we had hydraulic wires that gracefully and seamlessly lifted the poppies from floor to heavenly heights. In Cape Town, we had humble fishing wire swung over a ceiling beam, with faithful volunteers trying to gently raise them without too much jerking. We made sure the volunteers had gloves, so the wires didn't cause bloodshed. Bloodshed wasn't on the run sheet! In London the production team had a wee meltdown because they didn't have a budget for hydraulic cranes, and they momentarily decided, "Sorry, can't do the poppies." Thank God for Josh, one of our creative directors from Sydney, who convinced them that wire *will* work, avoiding a coronary on my part. And in all fairness, they did find something in the budget (I love the can-do spirit), and those English poppies were spectacular!

And then in Kiev (#fav), unbeknownst to me, insanely dedicated girls hid under the stage on the last night and somehow manually wove the flowers heavenward. All was fine till the closing exhortation to "Go home and flourish" took longer than usual because we had to translate everything into Russian. Oh dear, their poor little arms nearly fell out of their sockets as they tried to hold the flowers steady. Tragically, I may have noticed some quivering poppies out the corner of my eye.

The things we do for love, right? God bless production, creative, and events teams (and everyone else for that matter) who make beautiful things materialize from almost nonexistent budgets, because that year by the grace of God so many from all around the world took up the challenge.

Look Around

As those gathered at the conference hugged one another and said their good-byes, as production crews stood ready to enter and dismantle the environment, the girls left with a memorable visual and a new resolve to make home the garden it deserves to be.

I won't pretend any one of us is getting it perfect 100 percent of the time, but that beautiful garden spoken of in Isaiah is taking shape. It's finding its full bloom, and a generation of girls, like flowers in a glorious cascading garden, are discovering what it is to be the stunning and magnificent planting of the Lord. Stir imagination with me for a moment.

Imagine the planet and the people. Imagine nations, cities, and then neighborhoods. Imagine *the darkened places of both public and private habitation.* Imagine the shadows that cloud lives and existence and eclipse the light. Imagine all that is spiritually and literally stark and barren, and then imagine our homes and our lives amid them breaking into glorious color and life. Imagine your home and your life and all it represents breaking into color. Well, I can only imagine that that would resemble an oasis in a dry and thirsty, parched and colorless land. This is what God is after.

The contrast is not for comparison or vainglory—the contrast is so that people can see that there is a better way in Christ. God's desire is that neither the planet nor our hearts be a wasteland.

The ancient prophet Habakkuk said, "*Look around you...* among the nations and see! And be astonished! Astounded! For I am putting into effect a work in your days [such] that you would not believe it if it were told you" (Hab. 1:5 AMP, emphasis mine).

Let's open our eyes and have a good look around at all that sur-rounds us—the rooms, the gardens, the vineyards of our lives, the neighborhoods, and the world that is ours to steward—and let's decide today what needs to be watered and tended.

Let's be, in our lifetime, the change-makers needed.

• twenty-three •

SUNSHINE, BALCONIES, AND PILGRIMAGE

(The Way)

There is a way that seems right to a man, but its end is the way to death" (Prov. 14:12 ESV).

In the everyday street language of the Message paraphrase, the same verse frames it like this: "There's a *way of life* that looks harmless enough; *look again*—it leads straight to hell. Sure, those people appear to be having a good time, but all that laughter will end in heartbreak" (emphasis mine).

Strong words, to say the very least. Heartbreak and a lost eternity in hell are not the heart of God for anyone; therefore, like any good parent, He extends endless warnings about life and wisdom. They're warnings that are not given in harshness or condemnation—or with the intent to kill all the fun of life—they're given because there are basically two ways to do life: One leads to life eternal, and the other leads to death eternal.

Atheists, agnostics, and God-haters tend to be fiercely antagonistic toward such statements, while fairly ordinary people (who for some reason appear not to process life further than what lies on the surface) are somehow content to meander through life not fully realizing that the way they're going is fraught with danger, with an ending that could be horrific. Christ came to point us in the right direction and frame our pilgrimage along the way with purpose and mission.

Land of Philosophers and Poets

The inspiration for this chapter began in Greece. Nestled on the Mediterranean, this land is poignantly connected to our story.

Greece is renowned for philosophers and poets, historic ruins and fabulous food. I never studied ancient history, but this nation that boasts thousands of islands, crystal waters, and sunsets to die for was the birthplace of democracy around 500 BC. What I knew of Greek culture as a young woman stemmed mostly from the migrants who brought color and European culture to Australia. We all grew up mindful of Con the grocer, the local Greek-owned fish-and-chip shop, and the occasional redbrick suburban home adorned with white columns and maybe a naked statue or two. And then of course the movie *My Big Fat Greek Wedding* put it all in perspective and brought no end of cultural delight to my friend Christine (whose maiden name was Caryofyllis). Yes, one of my all-time besties is a Greek. Her own story is one of glorious redemption, and she was the principal reason a few of us were in Greece in the European spring of 2013.

The Windows

It was a clear and beautiful morning. There had been a small window of a few days between the London and Kiev conferences where three of us decided to max the time with a whirlwind trip to Greece and Bulgaria in order to visit the A21 human-trafficking shelters. As you will have gathered, we had for many years helped raise awareness and resources for these initiatives through Colour, but my own busy schedule hadn't allowed me the opportunity to actually visit personally. So here we were, keen to see everything firsthand, excited to visit with the rescued girls, and open to whatever God wanted to say or do. Two of our film team from Sydney were with us, because we were hoping to capture testimony to share with everyone at home who helps support this work.

Our van pulled up outside what looked like a normal suburban residence. The security gate slowly opened and we drove in. I may have quickly grabbed a tissue from my bag because I knew I would probably cry when I met the girls. What happened in the moments following is like slow motion in my head. I stepped from the van onto the little path that led to the front door and was met with a sight that in all truthfulness simply epitomizes summer—however, it was a sight that will haunt me forever.

A front bedroom window was wide open, with a lace curtain gently blowing and billowing in the sunshine and breeze. In the fleeting seconds of walking past that window, in the fleeting seconds of noticing the small garden beneath, in the fleeting seconds before the front door was flung open with an explosion of squealing and joyful girls, the scenes of the night before flashed before my eyes. In stark contrast (like the stark contrast of the statistic on the screens alongside the cascading flowers), the freedom of these windows and what I had witnessed the night before tore my heart apart.

The previous evening, our A21 friends on the ground there had wanted us to see the brothels of Thessaloniki. Phil would drive us. He knew the area inside out because this was their mission field and backyard. In Sydney we have a red-light area called Kings Cross—it's urban and busy, interwoven with cafés, restaurants, and public thoroughfares. It resembles the red-light districts that I imagine in most big cities. I'm not delusional that these areas don't also harbor backstreets and dark allies, but what we encountered this night in Greece looked and felt quite different.

We drove to what looked like the outskirts of what may have been a shipping area. The road turned and led into an area that felt isolated and remote And then, for what seemed like block after block after block, we drove around and past endless boxlike buildings that boasted not much more than limited windows, ominous closed doors, and the infamous red light above the entrance. In an area where shadows disappeared into sheer blackness, we came across row after row of trucks parked side by side in a place recently rezoned as a truck stopover—where drivers supposedly sleep and take rest.

On one narrow intersection, Phil slowed our vehicle and we saw three or four young men enter a brothel. At another we saw a handful of young men exit, laughing and joking, with one nonchalantly doing up the fly zipper on his pants. A handful of Greek mamas in a lane watched us suspiciously. They looked like the sweet grandmothers you see on European postcards, but Phil jarred my reality by telling me that more than likely they were brothel madams—the ones who probably clean the room when the client is done, organize the girls, and take the money.

Upsetting Is an Understatement

As we drove away, everything was upsetting, not least the fact that we could actually drive away.

I climbed into my clean and relatively safe bed in the hotel, which was only a few kilometers away back in town, but I couldn't sleep for knowing that out my window, at that distant point where ocean and lights and darkness merged, girls were right now being abused and used. It was well past midnight, and apparently activity heightens after midnight.

Everything about *everything* was disturbing, but as I tried to sleep, the thing I couldn't budge from my mind was the windows. Every brothel had windows that were boarded up, with bars on them—no light, no life, no sunshine or air, just harsh boarded and barred windows.

Uninformed and ignorant mind-sets will say that prostitution is legal in Greece and that girls choose this lifestyle. I'm tempted to become scathing here, but I will resist the temptation. It's true that prostitution is legal in some places and it's true that prostitution has probably been around since before the ark, but don't be lulled into complacency by Hollywood movies or the few who apparently choose the profession. The facts remain that the industry has changed and it is being driven by unprecedented greed, corruption, and all that is inherently evil.

If these girls I'm speaking of here have chosen prostitution, then let's remove the boards, remove the prison bars, unlock the doors, and then let's capture them on film, turning up for work with a coffee in their hand. Let's chat as they catch the 7:00 a.m. bus home after a mandatory eight-hour shift, taking a quick shower and rest before heading off to school or an afternoon of fun with their girlfriends. No. We all know it isn't like this. For these poor darlings, their night shift looks very different, as does probably their day shift, as does the entire length and breadth of their captivity, should they actually survive the ordeal.

So I'm sure you can understand how I felt when I walked past the open window with the lace billowing in the sunshine and breeze. The contrast of freedom and captivity was glaringly obvious— sunshine, lace, and freedom versus darkness, bars, and captivity. Our fight for freedom and our need to never cease being our little sisters' keepers had come thundering home again.

Sunshine, Lace, and Stories

To finish the story of the pathway and lace windows, we didn't need to knock. The front door flew open and everyone on my side of the door was lavished with kisses and hugs. To be honest, I was momentarily stunned because I couldn't figure if the girls in this loud and delicious welcome party were the A21 shelter team or the girls themselves—we honestly couldn't tell who was who, which in itself tells a story.

We were ushered in and introduced to everyone in the hallway—a beautiful team of workers, some of whom I did recognize, of course, once the initial excitement subsided—and then a handful of beautiful and precious young women who were in care at that time. Obviously I can't share much of their stories, but allow me to carefully say that one young girl from Asia was sold by her brother for the brothels of the Greek island of Santorini. She had been in protection for six weeks and hadn't yet smiled, but one of the workers whispered in my ear, "Bobbie, today she smiles!"

As we sat at the kitchen table listening to whatever these young women wanted to share of their dreams and aspirations for the future, one little girl stole my heart because she so reminded me of one of our pastors at home. Our Kety is Bulgarian. She is extremely petite, with a gorgeous sense of humor, and came to Sydney to attend Bible college. She married one of our all-time favorite spiritual sons and they pastor one of our Aussie campuses. The little girl now sitting beside me in Greece was the image of Kety. She also was Bulgarian. She was maybe sixteen, as pretty as a picture, and as I sat there watching her, I could not fathom how a man can visit a brothel, have sex with a child, and not know that something is inherently wrong with this picture.

The girls around that kitchen table were like little children because, for the most part, they were. They were excited to show us their rooms and their belongings, and had made handcrafted jewelry and handwritten cards for us. One of the team mothers shared that the younger girls recover faster. Once trust and safety are sensed, and once they get through the initial trauma period, their childlike heart allows the pain to be dealt with, unlike some of the older girls whose scars run deep and whose healing takes longer.

Laughter amid the Pain

These girls may be scarred literally, but they often don't lose their sense of humor. I am jumping stories, but on this same trip to Greece, we drove over the border and also visited the Bulgarian A21 transition home. As I walked into the hallway of this home, I extended my hand to one of the older girls, smiled, and gently said, "Hi, I'm Bobbie." Straight back at me she said, "Hi, I'm Julia Roberts" (of *Pretty Woman* movie fame), to which I may have spontaneously burst out laughing and said, "Well in that case, I'm Richard Gere" (not funny, but funny). She was delightfully hilarious. Of course, the cigarette burns on her arms and body and her horrific story of endless abuses weren't, but she was.

I'm intentionally adding a little warmth here, because these stories are intense and heartbreaking, yet somehow these girls survive and allow humor to help them. It's also a powerful reminder that they're girls just like us, or like our daughters and their friends. The Bible does say that laughter and cheerfulness are as medicine to a crushed and broken soul, and my small experience in and around these beautiful survivors has proven His Word to be true (see Prov. 17:22).

On the same day we visited the Bulgarian home, another young lady was asked to share her story of escape. She was sporting a leg in plaster that was resting affectionately on the knee of the shelter-house mom. As we respectfully and quietly listened, she told how she was taken by her traffickers to a hotel or apartment room where five foreign men were waiting. Not one or two, but *five*. Needless to say, they had their way with her. The men then fell asleep in another room, probably from alcohol and too much gang-like sex, I would imagine.

Our little angel saw her opportunity. A window was open and it led onto a small balcony. It was now or never. With bated breath, we all leaned in. She then said words to this effect: "I quietly climbed out onto the balcony but it was quite a way down...I had to jump, it was my only opportunity...so I thought...I better do some limbering up, stretching exercises." Okay, at that point the entire room burst into laughter (not least Julia Roberts). It was probably more of a nervous laugh on our part, but because the wee lass telling the story burst into laughter telling us, it somehow gave everyone else permission to do likewise.

Can you imagine this scene? Five drunken despots inside; traffickers probably waiting for a phone call to pick up the girl because the five have finished with her; an open window; a balcony...and a captive girl stretching, warming up, lunging up and down before she literally lunged to freedom. She jumped and she (of course) broke her leg, hence the plaster cast, but (hallelujah) she also escaped!

I'm sure heaven cheered when she landed, and thank God someone was on the ground to facilitate rescue and recovery. They may not have been there to catch her literally, but she is now caught up in the love of God, which if she can move forward with her life, will never fail her. If that girl ever reads this story, then, sweetheart, I pray I did it justice. Please forgive me if I didn't, but for the record you are one brave girl and I know people will be inspired by your courage.

Acceptable in His Sight

Isaiah 58 shows us the kind of Christianity that is acceptable in the sight of God. The King of heaven is not impressed with empty obligation or religious pomp and ceremony. Sometimes the things we think are *so* important are not on His priority list for the earth.

Each year I usually take a moment to revisit these words with the girls before we launch into our "Be the Change" sessions. It's so important that our focus remains pure and that we never wander from the path He has ordained, because the lives of these girls (and the many others I've sought to write about) are hinged to our responses. And may I say, every time I open my Bible to share these verses from Isaiah, I sense His presence draw near. It's proof to me that they're as applicable today as when they were first scribed. My prayer as you also read and absorb them is that they'll bring new life and clarity to all you're being called to.

Is not this the kind of fasting I have chosen: to loose the chains of injustice and untie the cords of the yoke, to set the oppressed free and break every yoke?

Is it not to share your food with the hungry and to provide the poor wanderer with shelter—when you see the naked, to clothe them, and not to turn away from your own flesh and blood?

Then your light will break forth *like the dawn*, and your healing will quickly appear; then your righteousness will go before you, and the glory of the LORD will be your rear guard.

Then you will call, and the LORD will answer; you will cry for help, and he will say: Here I am. If you do away with the yoke of oppression, with the pointing finger and malicious talk, and if you spend yourselves in behalf of the hungry and satisfy the needs of the oppressed, then *your light will rise in the darkness*, and your night will become like the noonday.

The LORD will guide you always; he will satisfy your needs in a sun-scorched land and will strengthen your frame. You will be like a *well-watered garden*, like a spring whose waters never fail.

Your people will rebuild the ancient ruins and will raise up the age-old foundations; you will be called Repairer of Broken Walls, Restorer of Streets with Dwellings. (Isaiah 58:6–12, emphasis mine)

Such beautiful and divine promise in each line. Two chapters along, Isaiah 60 is equally powerful and reveals that as we live in the power of all these surrounding chapters, His light, which leads to salvation, will arise upon the likes of you and me. If that isn't an invitation to destiny, an incitement to commit to journey to the very end of all He has for us, then I don't know what is.

Hearts Set on Pilgrimage

Why is there such a battle for this way that simply leads to life? Why does genuine Christian faith so often encounter contempt and hatred? Why do people who genuinely encounter Jesus Christ as Lord suddenly then encounter opposition from those who should rejoice that they've found meaning in life? I know my own relatives gave me a hard time, and my best friend (whom I'd known since the first day of elementary school) cornered me a few weeks into my conversion and made me choose between her and faith. We were on bicycles outside my house. I remember looking at her and saying, "Friend, it's not that I don't choose you, but of course I need to choose Jesus." She obviously didn't understand—she turned away and literally rode out of my young life that afternoon.

Why do genuine Christ-centered churches and genuine Christian leaders who give their lives for the betterment of others encounter persecution somewhere in the journey? Why? Because we're dealing with truth that has the capacity to bring true freedom. We're dealing with a world system that in some corners of society is vehemently anti-Christ, and we are dealing with unseen forces in heavenly realms that despise the Savior and are fiercely opposed to people finding Him and, therefore, their way home.

Zion is where we are all headed. In both everyday and romantic language, we're men and women, sons and daughters, pilgrims and travelers, explorers and soldiers on a journey home to heaven—to a place that an archangel-enemy once knew and lost and is hell-bent on sabotaging for the rest of us. Zion is described as a place where absolute peace and justice prevail. In ancient times, it was literally the city of God in Jerusalem, but today (for those of us still earthside) it is a city within our hearts and a powerful hope that draws us onward.

Psalm 84 speaks of those whose hearts are set on pilgrimage. It tells of a people who are homesick for heaven and who go from strength to strength, turning places of despair into places of blessing. It tells of a people whose faces shine with His gracious countenance and whose shields of spiritual armor glisten in the sun. It's a magnificent Psalm and in all honesty it is how I see the church (and this Sisterhood) in these latter days—a magnificent body of people carving their way home and gathering as many as they can along the way. From the desperate places on any continent in this world to the urban and suburban streets of any nation and city, there are people walking in either of two directions. They're busily on their way, but to where?

Two young men in our church wrote a song called "Arise," and my son Joel sings it on the album *Zion*. Perhaps I just love hearing his raspy voice sing it, or perhaps the lyrics are truly prophetic. They speak of the sacred thing, the sacred truth that we each hold and that we each carry through life:

Explorers and soldiers in you and in I
Searching and fighting till love is realized . . .
The fight we're in has already been won . . .
We're closer to heaven than we'll ever know . . .
Arise, for the kingdom has come
Arise for the kingdom has come.
"ARISE," HILLSONG UNITED, 2013

Zion is but a heartbeat away. Heaven is closer than we'll ever know. The days are darkening and a cloud of gloom is descending on those without hope, yet the Bible so clearly says that the glory of God upon His people in these latter days will be brighter than ever before. That light will become an irresistible beacon in the darkness and a lantern to light the way home.

As the verse opening this chapter reads, "there is a way that appears to be right, but in the end it leads to death" (Prov. 14:12). Therefore, it is incumbent on those of us who know there is a better way to shine and excel in calling and labor like never before, because people are too fabulous, wonderful, and precious to be lost.

twenty-four

SHE IS ONE, SHE IS MANY

(The Epilogue—From a Whisper to a Shout)

As I seek to bring this book to conclusion, I want to thank you for staying the distance with me. My publishers said that in many ways this book is a memoir—a record of events by someone having personal knowledge, an essay on a learned subject. I don't pretend to know everything there is to know about life; however, I have tried to capture the heart and spirit of something that I believe heaven has waited a long time for. If we were to study the pages of history and observe the women and sisters who have gone before us, it's not incorrect to say that the girls have come a long way.

Our Origin Is More Clear and Accepted Than Ever Before

Women are not beneath, behind, or secondary. We are worthy of honor, and even though Eve may have taken the apple, we are not responsible for the demise of humanity. When it comes to womanhood, we all know the world is not perfect and that pockets of humanity still linger in the dark ages, but for so many of us, the barriers have been broken and the walls have been torn down. As women, we've been correctly welcomed alongside, and the planet is a better place because of the contribution of the feminine heart, soul, and mind.

The Father holds no prejudice toward us, and there will be many an occasion in the days ahead when the girls will be front and center of His church and at the forefront of His purposes, helping to lead the charge and achieve all that is needed in this world.

As Women, We've Grown in Stature

Being human is an endless learning curve, but as women we've come of age on so many levels. We're learning to be truly comfortable in our skin, and we're realizing that there is a mantle and calling that is ours alone to wear. Many years ago, when I was a young woman, unsure of myself yet sensing destiny upon my life, another woman gently whispered and prophesied in my ear. She said, "Wear the mantle, and wear it with ease...Let it fall all around you and be comfortable in it."

It may sound cliché, but there is no one like you. Every man, woman, and child is created in the image of God, with works prepared and ordained for us to achieve from before the foundations of the earth (see Eph. 2:10). We either believe this or we don't—we either believe that we are created gender-equal with a world to influence and rule in together, or we don't. So if we *do*, let's relax into it and get on with the job of working alongside one another in the grand scheme of God's master plan for the earth (see Gen. 1 and 2).

Don't let anyone tell you that you are not included or able. Wear the mantle of your calling with ease—allow it to fall around you, and be comfortable in who you are. Don't ever doubt that you are able—because you're not able—but with God's Spirit working in and alongside, and with God's Word framing your every move, you will grow into the stature needed. Allow Him to redeem you and grow you into all He has designed.

There is a stunning prayer in Psalm 144 that says, "May our sons in their youth be like plants full grown, our daughters like corner pillars cut for the structure of a palace" (Ps. 144:12 ESV). I believe God's desire is that His daughters become magnificent pillars of strength in society, contributing to the depth, diversity, and wonder of this fabulous world we all call home. Pop stars may write songs about being royal, and Hollywood may make movies about palaces and princes, but you and I in Christ really are royal, with every right to the courts of heaven and the authority bestowed.

The Girls Are Learning to Be Brave

Brave women run in this family. It's an everlasting family that stretches from creation to the end of time and beyond. With the help of God's ever-present and willing Holy Spirit, a vast number of girls today are choosing to add their story to the ancient lineage of sisters whose stories have preceded us. We're learning the art of exchange—our lack for His abundance, our fear for His faith, our timidity for His boldness. Like our friend Christian in the famous allegory of The Pilgrim's Progress, we're learning that "the lions are chained" and there is nothing to fear. The Bible teaches that perfect love casts out all fear, and perfect love is found in Jesus. The enemy, adversary, and accuser (in whatever form he takes) can roar as much as he likes, but while Christ resides within, the roar has no power.

And Finally, We Are Finding Our Voice

Proverbs 31 instructs that we must open our mouths for the rights of those who have no voice.

This story began with a whisper—a still, small voice within that encouraged me to step beyond my fears and containment and make a stand for something greater than myself. I am not so presumptuous as to think that my whisper has been the only whisper in history. I think my Father has whispered many things to many daughters down through time and history, but for me the whisper was real. It lifted me beyond what I knew in the natural and compelled me into places that I can only say have been part of His divine will for my life and others'. The fruit bears witness that what I heard was indeed what He said.

The miracle of this modern day, "for such a time as this" (Esther 4:14), is that the whisper has resonated with many and become a shout—a ripple-effect shout of radical change and tangible hope for multitudes around the world. It is being heard in the far corners of the earth, from the suburbs of Sydney, Australia, to the bustling streets of cities and villages across the continents of this planet.

The Sisterhood cannot be reduced to an event or conference, or even a new wineskin within the church. It's all of these and a whole lot more. The true spirit of Sisterhood relates to the feminine heart realizing that she is truthfully a daughter of the Most High God, fashioned perfectly in His image and invited into intimate relationship with Him. When a woman awakens to that, she lives and walks differently, and everything about her life affects others.

And So, to That End, We Are Many

The story encompasses thousands. It's the story of thousands of women, tracking their way through time and history with endless stories to tell of God's amazing grace and goodness. It's Psalm 145 in motion—one generation telling its great works to another.

In Psalm 68:11, the Amplified version declares that the Lord will give the word of power, and the women who will bear it and publish it will be a great host. Not all translations frame these verses in a feminine context, but my much-loved Amplified version does. I was in Kiev a number of years ago (back when I met Lora in the hallway) and had the honor of meeting an American missionary who had lived in Moscow for twenty years at that point. We invited her to sing, and when she did, her operatic style transported us into what felt like another time in history. She was lovely—and as an aside, I remember her gently reprimanding us all for speaking too quickly: She told us that, no matter how clever or profound our sermon was, if we didn't slow down and allow the interpreters time to translate, the message of heaven would be lost to those listening. Point taken, we all slowed down.

She heard me share from this passage in Psalms and approached me afterward. With great kindness, she told me that I had shared the spirit of these verses perfectly. I leaned into what she was saying. She told me that "the scribes of Jerusalem" had told her that these verses in Psalms were Messianic and that when we see great hosts [plural] of women arising around the world, with the power, anointing, and authority of Christ upon them, it could well be indicative of His pending return.

My Prayer

The Bible teaches that it is not wisdom to predict Christ's return. However, it is wisdom to read the signs of the times—and the signs tell us that we are living in both amazing and perilous days (see Acts 2).

My prayer is that we will all live in a manner that prepares a way for our King's return and the immense harvest at hand. My prayer is that the church will rise to her full stature with everyone in place—men, women, children, and youth—all poised and positioned and playing our part in the greatest love story of all time. My prayer is that the potential within the daughters will not be quenched and that together we can make Him proud at every bend and curve of this journey. My prayer is that you'll be blessed beyond measure, and that the words in this book will inspire and ignite what is truly within you.

My husband often says the best is yet to come. And indeed it is. It doesn't matter what the past has served you—the future is always better, and especially better when we know that Someone divine and magnificent waits for us.

I spoke a message to the girls at our 2014 gathering called "Love Is on the Way." It stemmed from verses in the book of Jude and a little "night-season moment" on a snowy mountainside in California. As I lay in the darkness of the room with my beloved husband sleeping peacefully beside me, I felt God inspire courage and confidence with the words, "Relax, everything's going to be all right; rest, everything's coming together; open your hearts—love is on the way!" (see Jude 1:2 MSG).

At the time, I thought my Jesus was stilling my anxious heart in context of workload and responsibility. However, I came to understand in the months following that He was stilling my heart in context of our pilgrimage as a couple and as a church. In what was a year of profound blessing, expansion, and unforced favor, we also encountered a year fraught with challenge and heightened opposition. What I learned that year was that my Savior truly waits for me down this pathway and road called life. He is in each new day. He is at every intersection of life. No bend or curve or dangerous encounter takes Him by surprise. My entire confidence took newfound rest in the knowledge that He has gone ahead, has everything under control, and has mercy and grace in readiness for the countless new days that will dawn over our lives.

My only need is to follow Him—to follow hard on His heels and stay close within His shadow. The beatitudes in Matthew 5 record Jesus climbing a mountain in order to open His heart and teach His disciples the rhythms of life. The Message translation describes those following as His committed climbing companions. My desire is to be found among those climbing companions. When He climbs, I want to climb with Him. When He draws aside to speak, I want to be among those who draw aside to listen. When He faces the enemy, I don't want to be counted with those who run for cover, but rather I want to stand confidently, knowing the authority He has invested within me. If and when He leads through wilderness places or through valleys unknown, I want to follow, knowing that He has me covered.

My prayer is that you'll walk in this same confidence and that together we will navigate life with magnificence. Many years ago, I wrote these words into the Colour journey: "She smiles at the future, lives life magnificently, executes justice on the earth, and places value upon humanity."

The mandate hasn't really changed; it has just come of age.

So wherever life takes you and whatever life deals you, don't forget to smile upward. It delights heaven, unlocks your heart, makes a way for His goodness, and irritates the pants off the devil. And if it is within your power (which it is, sweetheart), live life magnificently. Your example will inspire and bear fruit that will reach far into eternity. Imagine that.

And stand with those who live on the side of justice. Be the Psalm 45 girl who rides on triumphantly for the cause of justice and peace. And never lose sight of how beautiful it is to advocate for those who need to know they're loved and not forgotten. Isaiah 52:7 says, "How beautiful on the mountains are the feet of those who bring good news"—good news of acceptance, good news of embrace, good news of value and worth, good news that all is well.

The invitation was always to place value upon womanhood, in order that womanhood can arise and place value upon humanity. Never underestimate the wonder of what risen women can do when merely believed in . . . "Bobbie . . . tell them that there is a God in heaven who believes in them."

So on that note I leave you for now. You are altogether lovely. I may not know you personally and I may never meet you this side of eternity, but that's not important for now. What's important is that we understand we have been called by name and are graced for such a time as this. As ancient Esther's story teaches, if we don't rise up, where will deliverance come from?

Be safe and be blessed till we meet again—the journey continues . . .

Always and forever,

Bobbie

May the LORD answer you in the day of trouble;
May the name of the God of Jacob defend you;
May He send you help from the sanctuary,
And strengthen you out of Zion;
May He remember all your offerings,
And accept your burnt sacrifice. *Selah*
May He grant you according to your heart's *desire*,
And fulfill all your purpose.
We will rejoice in your salvation,
And in the name of our God we will set up *our* banners!
May the LORD fulfill all your petitions.
Now I know that the LORD saves His anointed;
He will answer him from His holy heaven
With the saving strength of His right hand.
Some *trust* in chariots, and some in horses;
But we will remember the name of the LORD our God.
They have bowed down and fallen;
But we have risen and stand upright.
Save, LORD!
May the King answer us when we call.

(PSALM 20 NKJV)

ACKNOWLEDGMENTS

Family is truly everything, and I am blessed to be sharing life with so many astounding people who have added to the richness of bringing this story to the page.

I want to thank my amazing husband, Brian. Without his gentle yet firm belief in me, I would never have stepped out twenty years ago to begin this journey. He has always believed in the potential of women, and his genuine example of releasing women into their vision, dream, and destiny has been an influencing benchmark for many around the world.

I want to thank my gorgeous children—Joel, Ben, and Laura. Like all young people they've each had their moments, but for the most part they have understood the calling on their parents' lives and have never resisted that calling. Our greatest joy is watching them love what is closest to our hearts, excel in their own calling, and take this kingdom message further than we could have ever hoped or imagined.

I am deeply indebted to our beloved church, Hillsong. Words are inadequate to describe this stunning company of people, who now span the globe. They passionately and selflessly live for a cause greater than themselves, and this story would not have happened without them, because in all truthfulness, it is their story. We say that Hillsong is not built on the gifts and talents of a few but on the sacrifices of many—therefore any eternal reward and fruit belong to them also.

And of course, my greatest gratitude goes to my God: "Thank You, Father, for allowing me the honor and privilege of bearing, carrying, and contributing to this message. Thank You, Lord Jesus, for trusting us with something so precious to Your heart. We will continue to give our finest, labor for the well-being of others, and in and through You, dear Spirit, we will finish what You have begun. You get the glory, Lord. Thank You, thank You, thank You."

BRIAN & BOBBIE HOUSTON

Brian and Bobbie Houston are the Senior Pastors of Hillsong Church, a church that is often referred to as "one house, many rooms". Hillsong has churches in 14 countries on five continents with the flagship campus based in Sydney, Australia. Brian and Bobbie are passionate about the local church and the potential within each individual who call Hillsong Church home.

Pastor Brian's infectious love for people and his empowering brand of leadership is beamed to millions of people weekly through his program, Brian Houston at Hillsong Television, and draws tens of thousands annually to Hillsong Conference in Sydney, London and New York City.

Pastor Bobbie Houston is passionate about seeing all people find Jesus as their Saviour and gain a revelation of their value in Him. She has redefined the face of 'women's ministry,' raising up a strong and capable company of women through a local Hillsong Sisterhood, global Colour Sisterhood and flourishing annual Colour Conferences that take place across four continents. Brian and Bobbie spend much of their time imparting and building the church across the globe and love family time with their 3 children and 6 grandchildren.

THE COLOUR CONFERENCE

The 'Colour Your World Women's Conference' started in 1997 and is hosted by Bobbie Houston and the global Hillsong Church team. It flows from the heart of Hillsong's local Sisterhood ministry where women from every age and walk of life gather. At its core, the conference exists to place value upon womanhood and champion the potential within women everywhere. Bobbie and the Hillsong team currently host this conference in Sydney, London, Kiev, Cape Town and the USA (NYC).

The COLOUR Conference is much more than an annual event that gathers thousands of women; it is an ever-growing global movement of everyday women seeking to create a stance for justice, change and influence. Our team labour to create an atmosphere that will refresh heart and soul and inspire transformation. Our desire is that worship, creativity and the presentation of God's Word (the Bible) will honour the King of heaven and cause faith to rise, enabling the enormous potential within to become reality. The conference is continually creating pathways for women to raise awareness and mobilize response.

The Colour story is one of "divine grace" and it's ability to find its way into the human heart and weave the story of God's great love into the lives of those seeking a better world.

"For God SO LOVED the world that He gave His one and only Son – that whoever believes in him shall not perish, but have eternal life" (John 3:16)

FOR MORE INFORMATION VISIT COLOURCONFERENCE.COM

THE SISTERHOOD

'Sisterhood' is a term that reflects the heart and spirit of a rising generation of women around the world. Age, background and culture are proving no barrier to this emerging and beautiful movement. Everyday women from every corner of the earth are leaning into the revelation that they are indeed daughters of a living and loving God, and that as His daughters, they carry a capacity and authority to bring change in an ever-challenging and needful world.

Defined by genuine empathy, the influence of this host of world-changers is being felt in local and global contexts - from endeavours that bring care to the fragile in local communities, through to the global issues of human trafficking and poverty.

At the core of Sisterhood is a message of value, and a genuine desire to 'unite in friendship and cause', in order to bring hope where hope has been lost. The spirit of sisterhood is seen and felt in the fervent prayer of thousands of women who faithfully uphold nations where injustice and darkness rage out of control. It is seen and felt in young women being inspired by the wisdom and grace of their mothers and the women ahead of them in this journey of life. It is seen and felt in the relentless networking of everyday girls in their local neighbourhoods and in places of influence, as they raise awareness and find solutions for the suffering, forgotten and abused of this world.

There are many pages and chapters within the story of God's daughters on the earth, and as the 'I AM SISTERHOOD' declaration states, we find ourselves in our own 'here and now' with more pages yet to be written and experienced. For insight into the breadth of the Colour Sisterhood, go online and peruse through the various humanitarian initiatives and 500 PROJECT responses. Together we can make a difference.

COLOURSISTERHOOD.COM

MORE RESOURCE
AVAILABLE AT BOBBIEHOUSTON.COM

THE ROAD LEADS HOME
Film One (2013): **Everyday Women**
Film Two (2014): **Our Sister's Keeper**
Film Three (2015): **The Road Leads Home**

Three years ago I asked our gifted film team to produce a "trilogy of films" that would bring clarity to the heart of Colour and capture the true spirit of Sisterhood. Our hope was to inspire women to the greatness, possibilities and potential within us all. To that end we have featured these films each year within the Colour Conference and I know many have been deeply impacted - they are each unique, diverse and moving stories.

We offer these three films in the hope that they will resource you and your world to make a difference. My prayer is that this labour of love and investment on our part, will bless those in your world and bear fruit eternal. - *Bobbie Houston*

THE BRAVE SERIES
Brave Women Run In My Family

In this series Bobbie unpacks aspects of their story in a manner that draws from both their strengths and weaknesses and in a way that is applicable to our everyday modern lives. Understanding the landscape of their surroundings and times, helps us understand ours.

This series has been an all time favorite within the (Hillsong) Sisterhood. We are systematically working through the qualities of 40 amazing girls (the list is found in the back of the 2014 Colour Sisterhood Bible), whose lineage of grace has so much to teach us.

THE BRAVE SERIES
If My Journey Could Teach You Anything

Bobbie took a moment to punctuate the series (in late 2014) with some insight, perspective and wisdom from "her own journey" that now spans over 40 years in ministry with Brian, and over 30 years pastoring Hillsong Church around the world. We're confident you'll find applicable and heartwarming leadership dynamic in these two messages that will infuse you with strength to press on in a powerful way.

NEW BOOK FROM BOBBIE HOUSTON COMING IN 2017

For more information, resource and to stay up to date with Bobbie Houston, Hillsong Church and The Colour Sisterhood visit **bobbiehouston.com** or connect through social media below.

Follow Bobbie on Twitter: **@bobbiehouston** / **@coloursistahood**
Follow Bobbie on Instagram: **@bobbiehouston** / **@coloursisterhood**
Like Brian and Bobbie on Facebook: **fb.com/brianandbobbie** / **fb.com/coloursisterhood**

PODCASTS

Each and everyday, people are accessing free audio podcasts from Pastor Bobbie Houston. These messages are created to bring hope and encouragement to women young and old with practical and biblical teaching. Your work life, home life and relationships matter to God – and they matter to us. Join in with others from around the world to receive free teaching that will unlock and unleash you to your greatest potential.

To access and subscribe to these life-giving messages, search for "Bobbie Houston" in the iTunes Store or Podcast App.